Deep Joy

Reflections on Life

POEMS & PHOTOS BY TOM FINLAY
ILLUSTRATIONS BY URSULA CLIDIÈRE

ISBN: 978-1-7392299-0-0

Cover and interior design by meadencreative.com
First printing edition 2022.

Contents

Foreword

As my mind plays with what to write as a foreword for this beautiful treasury of poems and illustrations, Luciano De Crescenzo's words dance across my mind,

"We are each of us angels with only one wing, and we can only fly by embracing one another."

Tom and I started sharing, singing, and soaring together shortly after admitting our 'Closet Poet' identities to each other in a randomly chosen 'break-out' room. What began as an unexpected meeting has grown into a creative connection that continues to surprise, support, and challenge me.

What you see here as a collection of poems and illustrations, dear reader, have been perfectly timed wake-up calls, new reality-bubble-popping perspectives, safety in moments of fear and certainty in uncertainty for me. Tom's poetry has changed my thinking, opened new possibilities, and encouraged me, but most of all, whenever a new offering lands in my inbox, he reminds me to appreciate and connect to my own Deep Joy.

I met Ursula through Tom and loved her exuberance immediately! Before I knew it, I felt the encouraging power of a true Brave Voices supporter and advocate. If Tom encouraged me to share my own Brave Voice, Ursula encouraged me to stay playful and curious with surprise parcels of crafty fun and invitations back to myself arriving randomly in my post box.

Deep Joy is such an apt title for this volume. Open yourself up to it, dear reader, as perfectly timed invitations to connect to your own Joyful voice and you won't be disappointed.

Gillian Walter, Author of *Choir of Brave Voices. Creative Reflections for a Seasonal Journey of Self-Discovery*

John Keats wrote "A thing of beauty is a joy forever." Keats's words express for me the sheer beauty, rawness, and vitality of this new book from Tom and Ursula.

Tom and Ursula reach out to us from beyond the page – and from beyond time and space – to both inspire and touch us with their art as well as giving us balm, hope and solace in the midst of our complicated lives.

Their work together reaches the sacred reaches of our hearts and souls where we are both tender and where our boundless creativity also lies. This book speaks to our shared humanity, our shared human condition and what it means to be human. With Tom and Ursula by our side we are reminded that we are never alone. Thank you for daring to gift yourselves to us through the rich warp and weft of your beautiful work together".

Elaine Patterson, Author of 'Reflect to Create! The Dance of Reflection for Creative Leadership,
Professional Practice and Supervision

A Deep. Joyous. Melancholy. Surprising. One. Other. Both. My journey through *Deep Joy* has been filled with discovery – whether diving into Tom's beautiful poetry, drinking in Ursula's magnificent and playful watercolors, or experiencing the weaving together of their shared musings.

I am grateful that they have discovered each other, and that I have discovered this gem. This is an inspired work that begs to be explored over and over which I will do! Thank you for creating this gift for the soul!

Michael Rubell

It is a rare and beautiful thing when creative kindred spirits such as Ursula and Tom bring together the threads of their artistic talents and weave them so beautifully into a shared piece of work that is vibrant, vital, complementary, each with their own special and unique expression, that on these pages form something that sparkles with an energy of the sacred as well as joyful. It is a tribute to them both, to what is possible when we dream and a gift to us the readers.

Karyn Prentice, Author of *Nature's Way. Designing the Life You Want Through the lens of*
Nature and the Five Seasons.

Preface – Tom

This book emerged from two deep creative collaborations. The context for these collaborations was the Tapestry program run by Elaine Patterson and Karyn Fletcher.

I have written poems since my late 'teens but I had never previously considered sharing them more widely than with my close friends and family.

What changed was my experience of the Tapestry Diploma whose tag line is *cultivating and choreographing the rich tapestry of wholehearted creativity*. I owe so much to Elaine and Karyn and my fellow-participants on this diploma.

This programme created a stimulating environment, out of which emerged the collaborations referred to above; both of my collaborators were fellow-participants in the Tapestry Diploma.

Timewise, the first collaboration is with Gillian Walter. Our initial virtual encounter was in a five-minute break-out group consisting of the two of us. This brief link-up was the catalyst for a deeply enriching creative dialogue and collaboration which has continued ever since.

I was enthralled as Gillian began to share her poems and paintings with me. Her emerging theme of "Brave Voices" has had a profound and lasting effect on me.

Gillian enthusiastically urged me to share my poems more widely and features a poem "Blessing" in her own recently published book Choir of Brave Voices in which she lyrically expresses her support. The first line of this poem is.

"May you know the power of your words"

Gillian's continuing support can be gleaned from the foreword that she kindly agreed to write.

My second creative collaboration is with Ursula Clidière with whom I have co-authored this book. Ursula and I connected when meeting virtually in an exhibition of our Tapestry projects. Shortly afterwards we began to play at pairing my poems with her art and my photos.

In this regard, Ursula's role was very broad. Not only has she painted the wonderful illustrations to accompany and enhance many of my poems, but Ursula has also been responsible for selecting the optimum photo to accompany a poem. I took almost all my photos on the Erris Peninsula in Ireland's Northwest. This is a place for which I have a deep love and sense of belonging – my soul – home.

As we began to produce our 'pairings' we shared them with friends and colleagues who encouraged us to share them more widely. This encouragement and the support of our families has led to us publishing this book.

Tom and I both took part in a year-long "creative journey and pilgrimage" facilitated by a program (Tapestry by Elaine Patterson and Karyn Prentice) we both were enrolled in. The purpose of the program is to develop Bespoke Practices using creativity as catalysts for Practitioners. The journey included the exploration of our individual relationship with creativity, different media to express it, and how to use it resourcefully. Many program participants used the program as platform for sharing their creative product more broadly.

For Tom and I, our catalyst to a co-creation and broader sharing was a deeply moving Exhibition (aka "Graduation") ceremony- at this point, we directly engaged for the first time. Our third Exhibition team member, Trish Anastos, does need to be mentioned at this point as another integral member of a creative fusion taking place. What exactly happened between this creative fusion and the writing of the preface to this small publication, will not be traceable- yet it portrays the joy and flow of collaborating.

The fusion taking place at our Program Exhibition event allowed for creativity to emerge, and co-creation carried it forth – without questioning, judgement, or precontemplation. The co-creations – pairings – shared in this booklet ultimately show how two worlds, two persons quite unfamiliar with one another other than the thread of the Tapestry program, can deeply connect and dynamically create.

These pairings may represent tensions, juxtapositions and possibly, even contradictions. Tom offers poems from a long steady line, images that reflect his ties with Ireland while my creative products are more contemporary, eclectic- having called many places home while having learned through creation that home sits in the self. The pairings, or their individual components, may challenge, reinforce, inspire, soothe, comfort or they may also invite deeper reflection and resolution. We noticed that not one reaction or reflection to our collaboration was the same. It is our hope is that the pairings offer a reflective landing pad for the reader giving space, new or different thoughts, and insights.

Acknowledgements

My wife – Caroline (Love of My Life page 59) – has been steadfast in her encouragement and support, as have our four adult children Ellen, Patrick, Conor, and Rory.

Beyond family, my preference here is to acknowledge groups of people rather than naming individuals. This is because, as there have been so many people who supported me, by naming some, I would be excluding others.

The first group that comes to mind is the wider community of the Coaching Supervision Academy (CSA). In particular, the teaching faculty and my fellow-participants in the Diploma in Coaching supervision which concluded in October 2019. This was where I was first encouraged recently to share my poems more widely.

The next group are my fellow-participants in the Tapestry Diploma program which is already covered very fully above.

I would also like to acknowledge the support of my clients with whom, as appropriate, I have shared my poems and whose encouragement has been invaluable. Another group consists of the friends and working colleagues, with whom I have shared poems and who in many instances have reciprocated with their own creations. Many thanks to you all!

Finally, there is one other individual I do want to mention and thank, namely my creative Partner Ursula. My creative collaboration with Ursula continues to be a wonderful and enriching experience.

Tom Finlay

I owe acknowledgement to so many persons lending their support, encouragement, advice, and insights to us, to me. Always and always first, I want to thank my husband Thierry – had it not been for his unfaltering belief in me, his encouragement and partaking, peeking and candidly sharing, and embracing where the creative journey took me, this book may never have come into existence. Merci beaucoup, mon b!

Deepest thanks to Elaine Patterson and Karyn Fletcher for offering us such tremendous support and encouragement to explore creativity with the Tapestry program! I wish to thank my Café Trio, Feryal and Pirjo, for their support and giving so many sparks (from Haiku poems to Rumi), Gillian who became another creative Tapestry friend and who so generously shares so much of what she holds dear, to Trish who was part of both, the end of the Tapestry program and the beginning to this co-creation, Isa Down for all water color inspirations, to my acquaintances, friends and family, from way back and now, near and far, who have readily embraced this different side of me.

I am also thanking all those who expressed gratitude, support, surprise, or simply openness when receiving bits and pieces of our creative journey- you will never know how much your feedback, reactions, and sharing encouraged me and us to stay creative!

And of course, my deep thanks to my creative partner, Tom- each of us had probably some moments where the courage left us and here it was the steadfast, even feisty support we lent to each other that got us through!

Ursula Clidière

Poems

ILLUSTRATED WITH FLOWER PAINTINGS

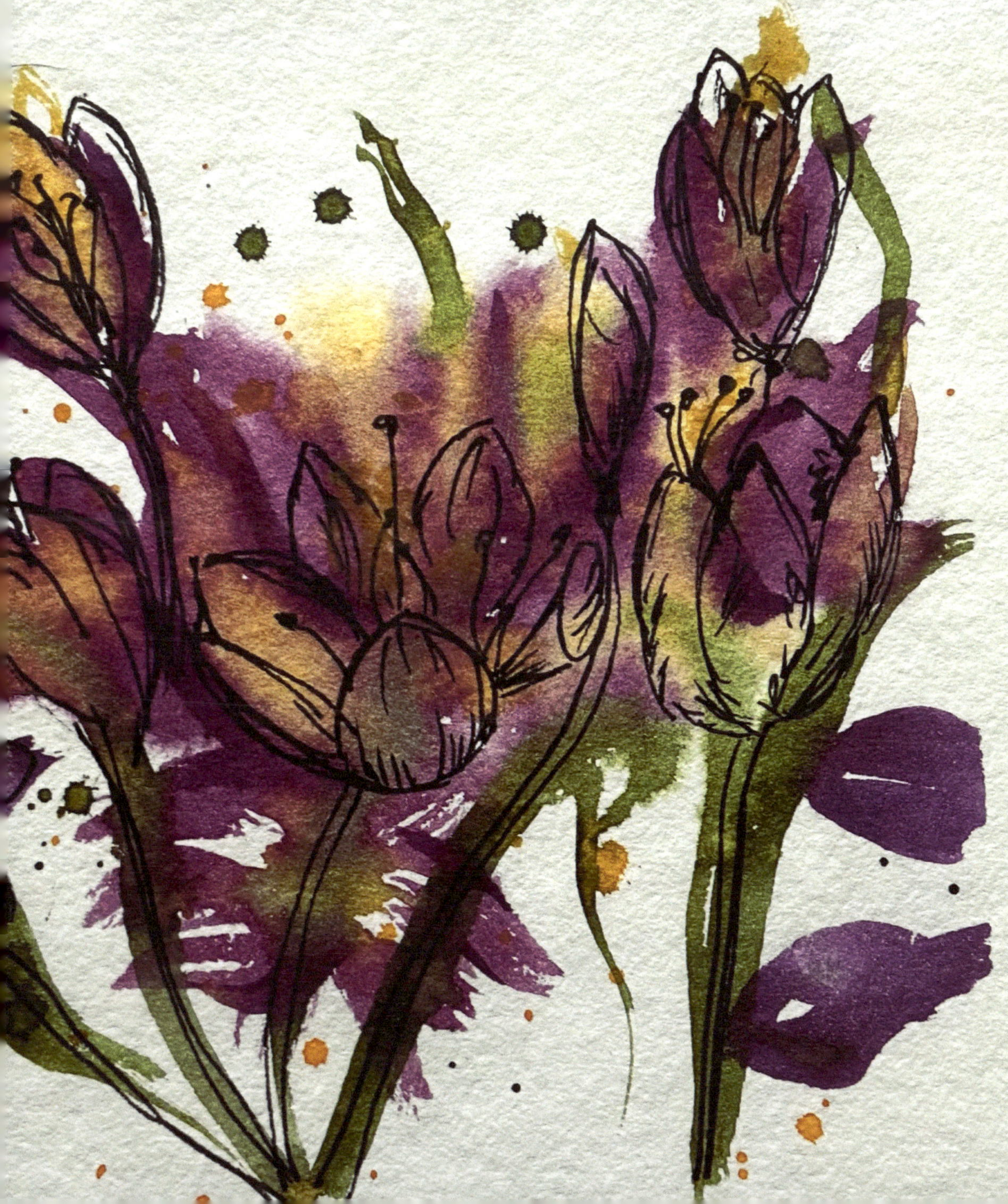

Snow Crocus

New life after
the dark winter
signpost to
the coming spring

Symbol of optimism
and belief
promises of growth
and warm sunshine

Yet the snow crocus
is complete
in its own space
and moment

13

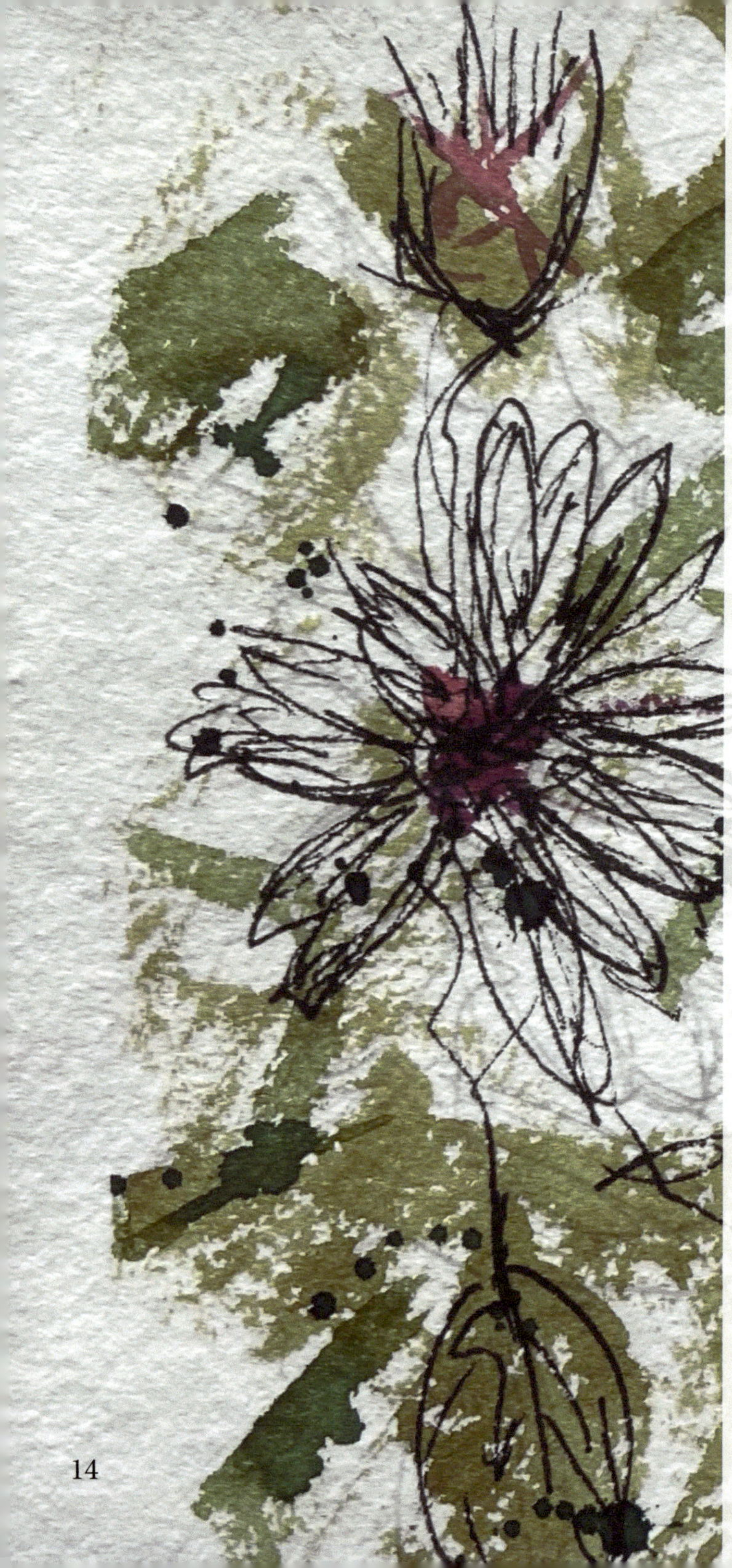

Meaning

The search
Is always
for meaning
to some
It comes
slowly
painfully
for others
it is there
from the start

Meaning gives life
hope grace
and blessings
are also
in the mix

For me
it was
always there
but only
emerged
as I fell
and got up
many times

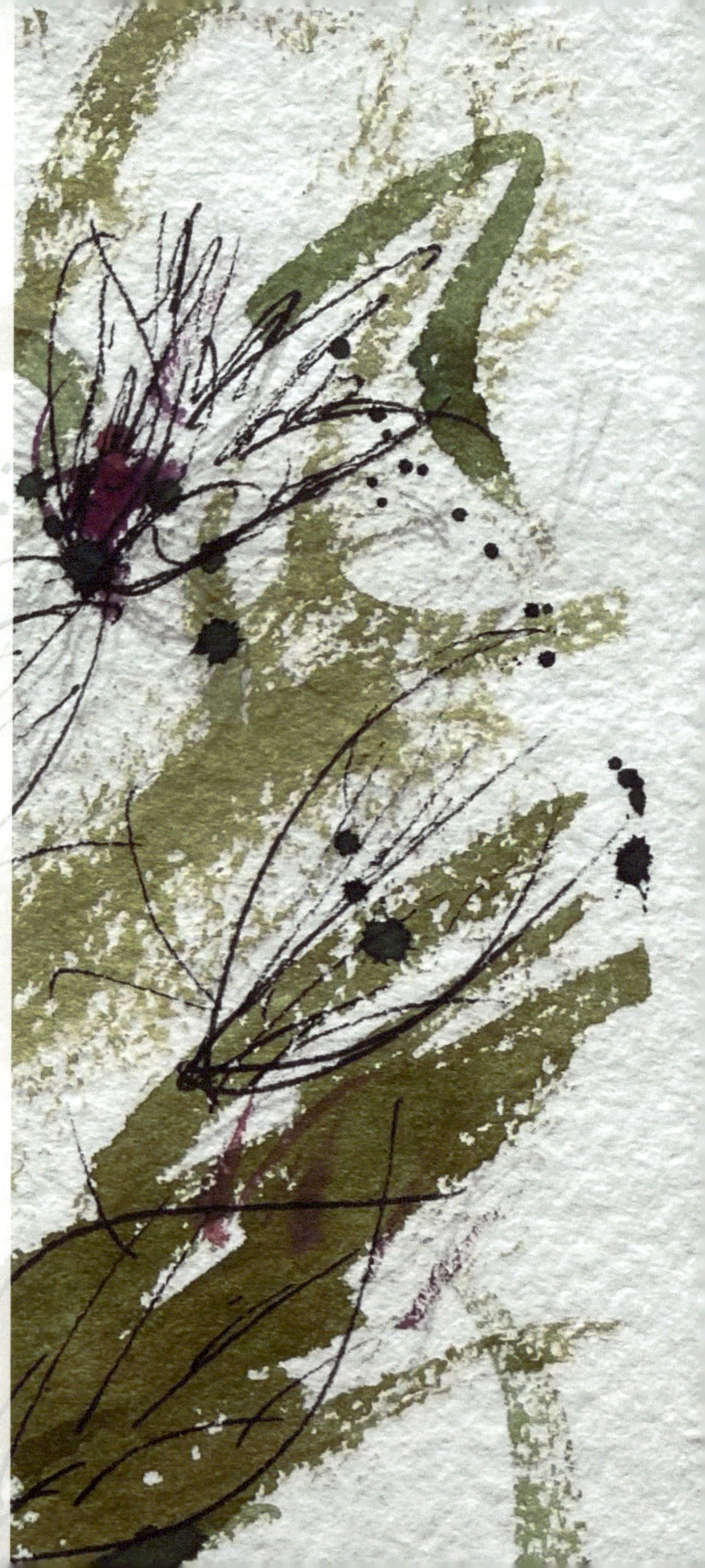

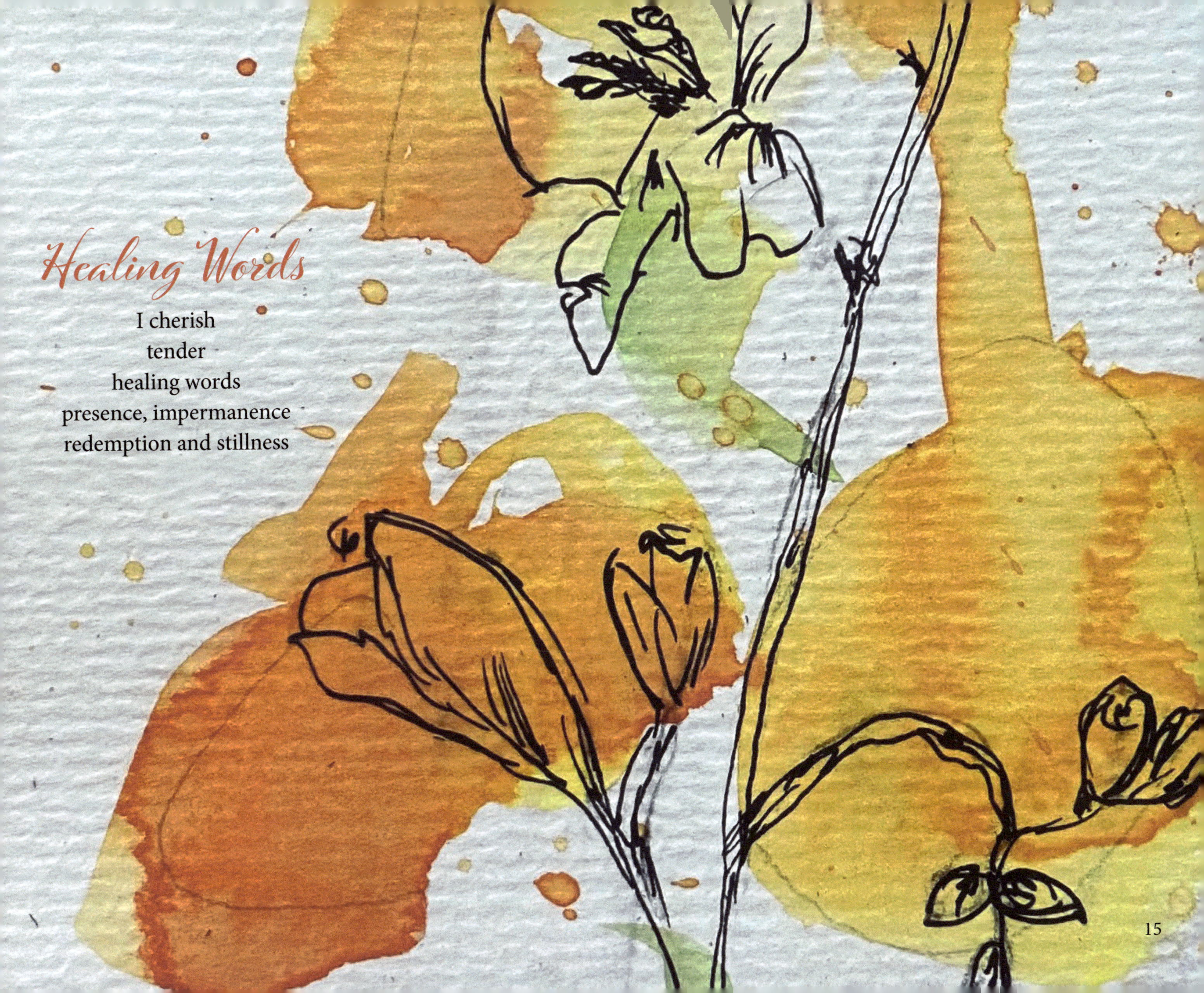

Healing Words

I cherish
tender
healing words
presence, impermanence
redemption and stillness

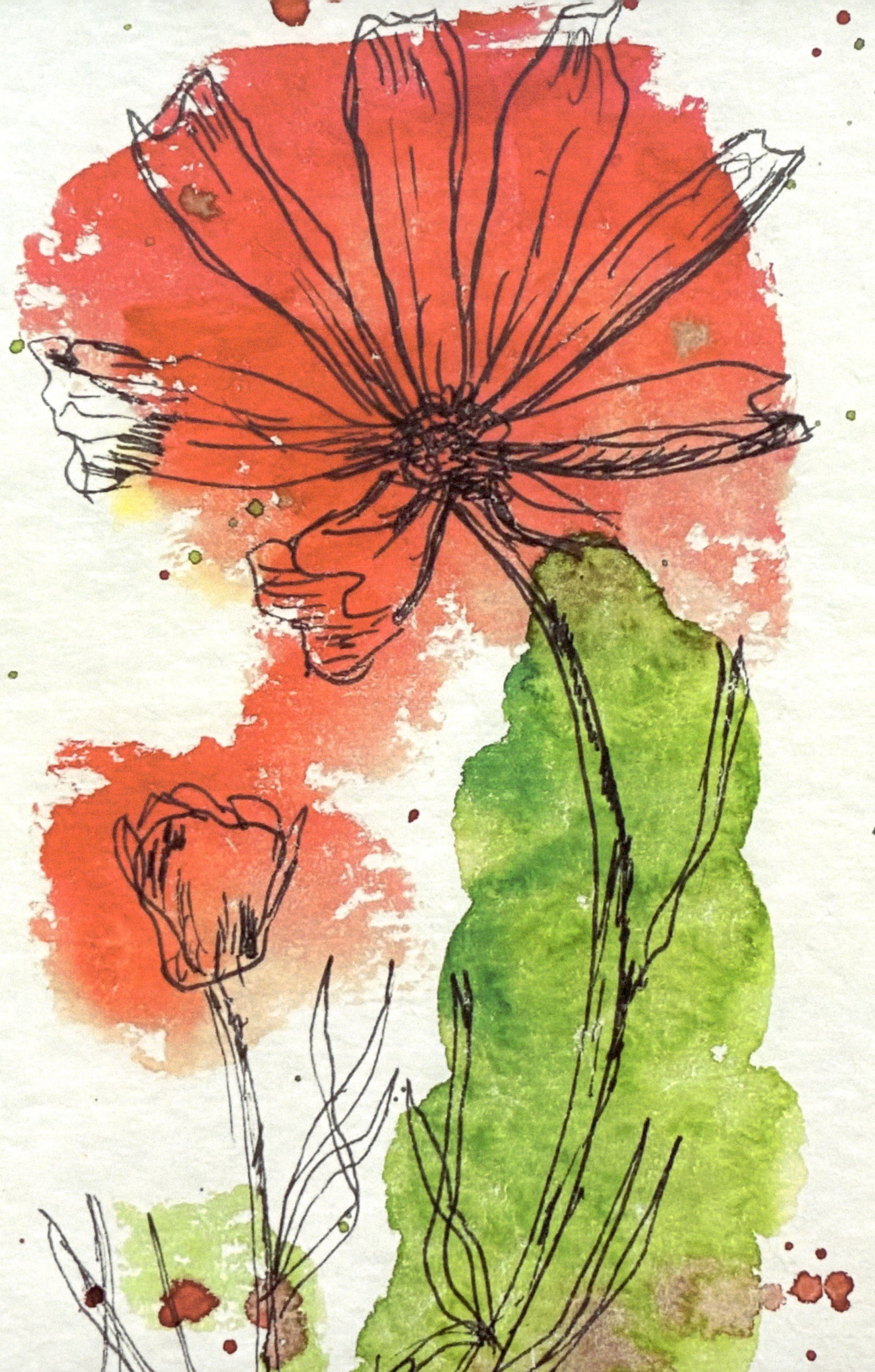

The New Day

Warmth and touch and beauty
hopes and plans
and Van the man
much talk and listening
growth and
some pain
as we step out
of old skins
to greet
the new day

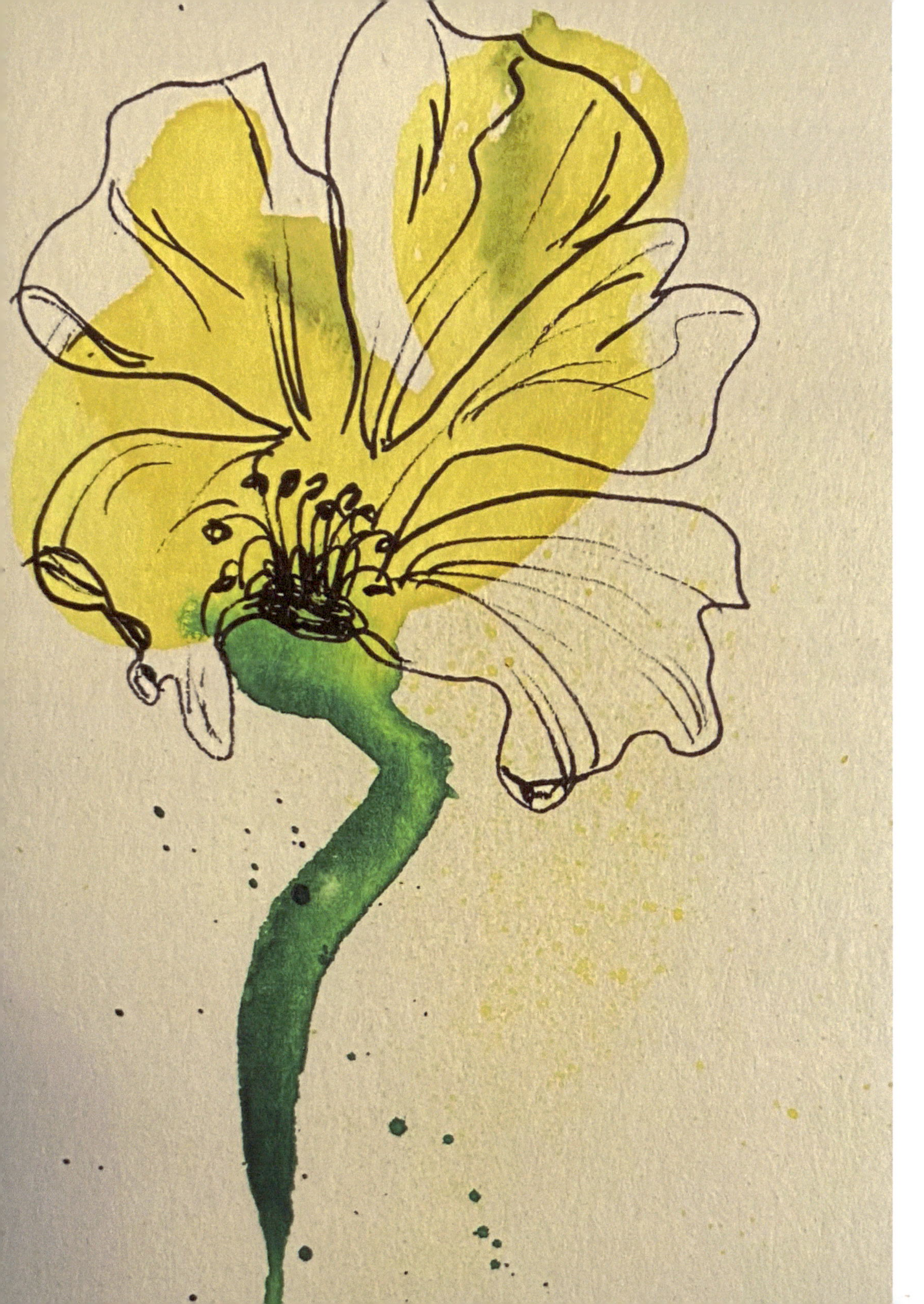

The Light

I have a friend
whom life
has kicked around
who has loved
and losing all
can smile
at trees and grass

I have a friend
whom rain
has battered
thunder shaken
and yet
who
loves the light

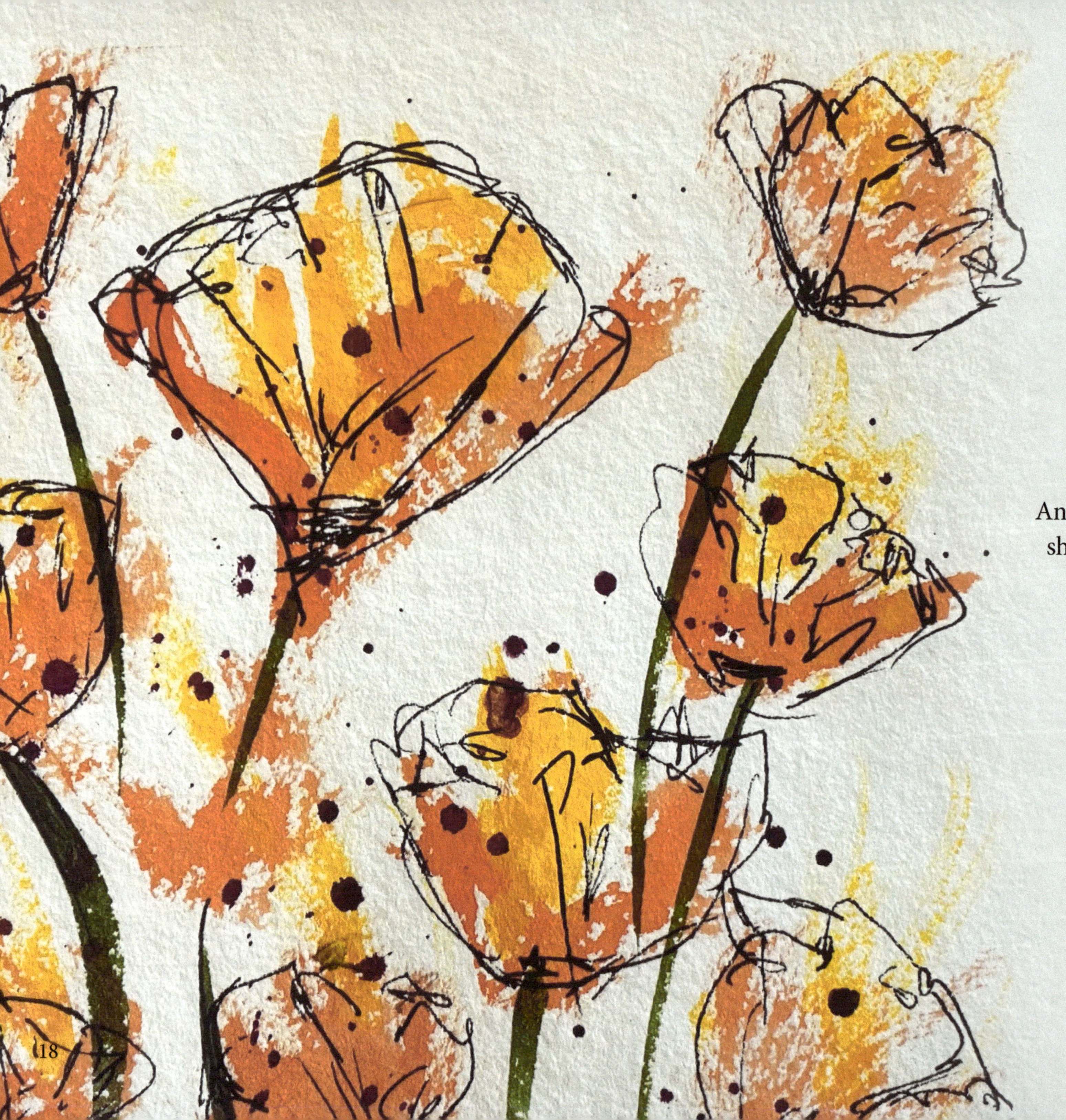

If

If every morning
we could shed
one skin
and start the day
more naked
yet more real

And watch our mirrors
shine a little stronger
and forget
to score to gain
to win

If we could
every morning
just begin

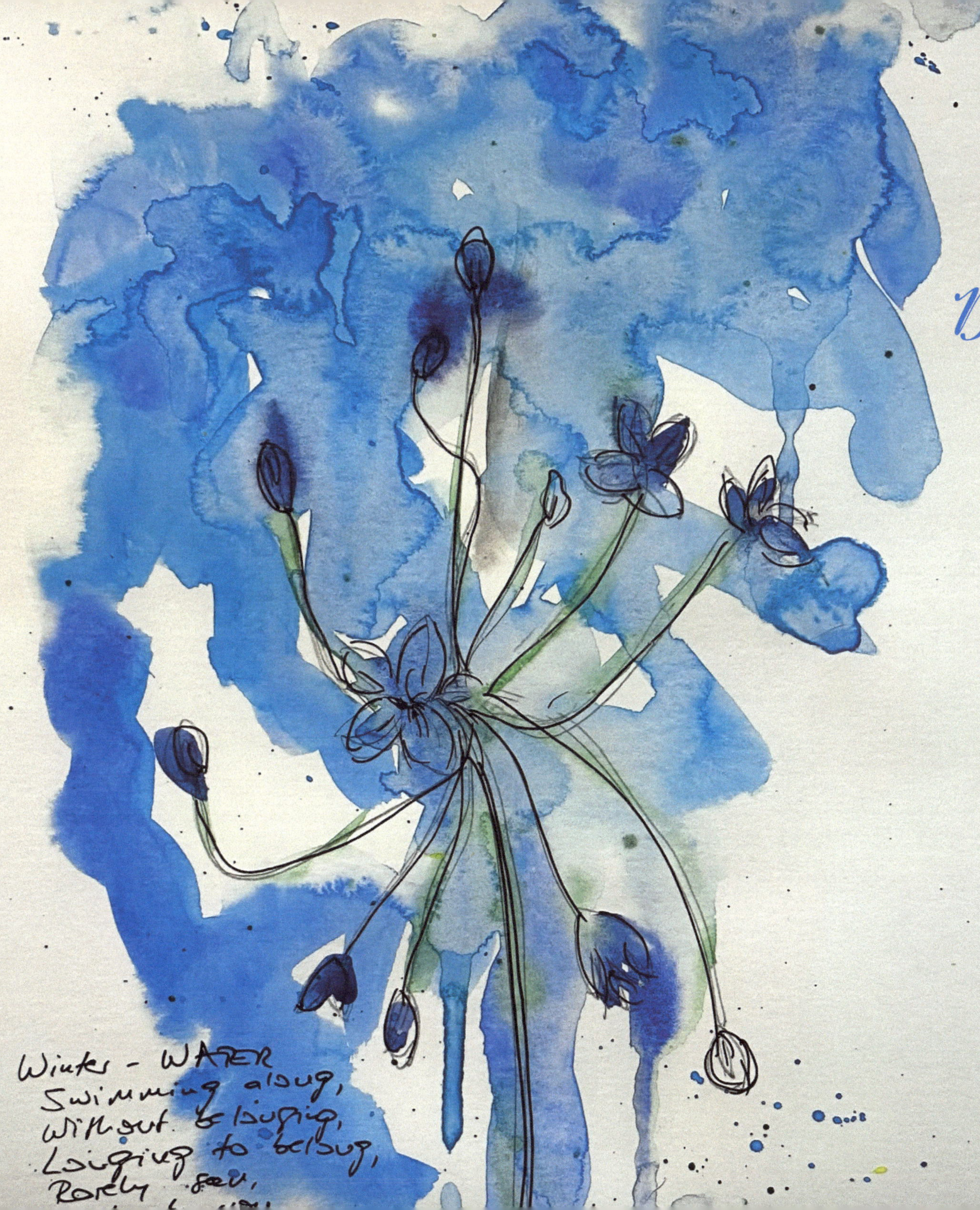

December 2017

Everything changed
healing is complete
I faced a test
came through
with tent poles
in place

Stillness
has taken hold
of inner space
words melt
Into a
warm silence
I breathe
that's enough

19

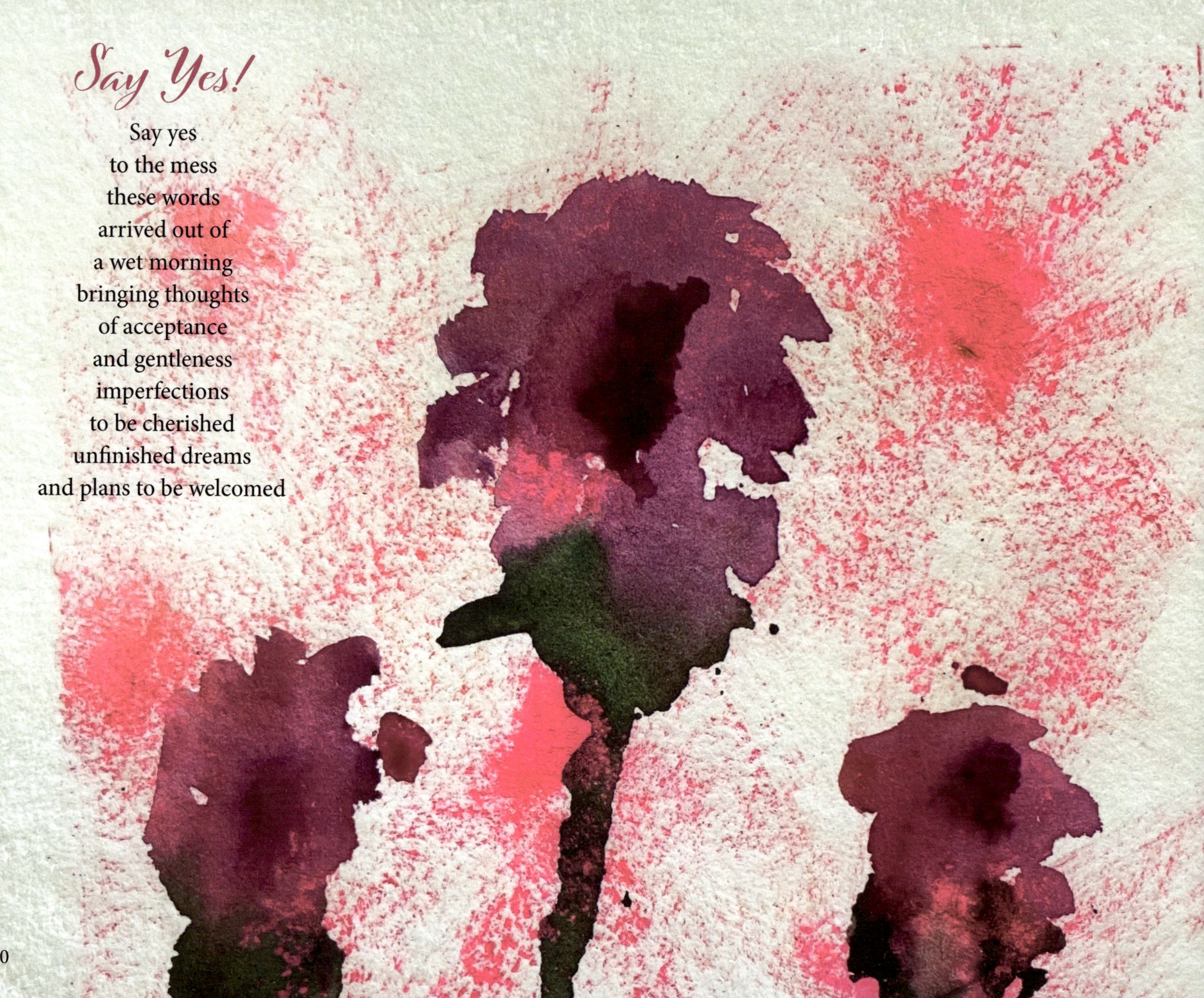

Say Yes!

Say yes
to the mess
these words
arrived out of
a wet morning
bringing thoughts
of acceptance
and gentleness
imperfections
to be cherished
unfinished dreams
and plans to be welcomed

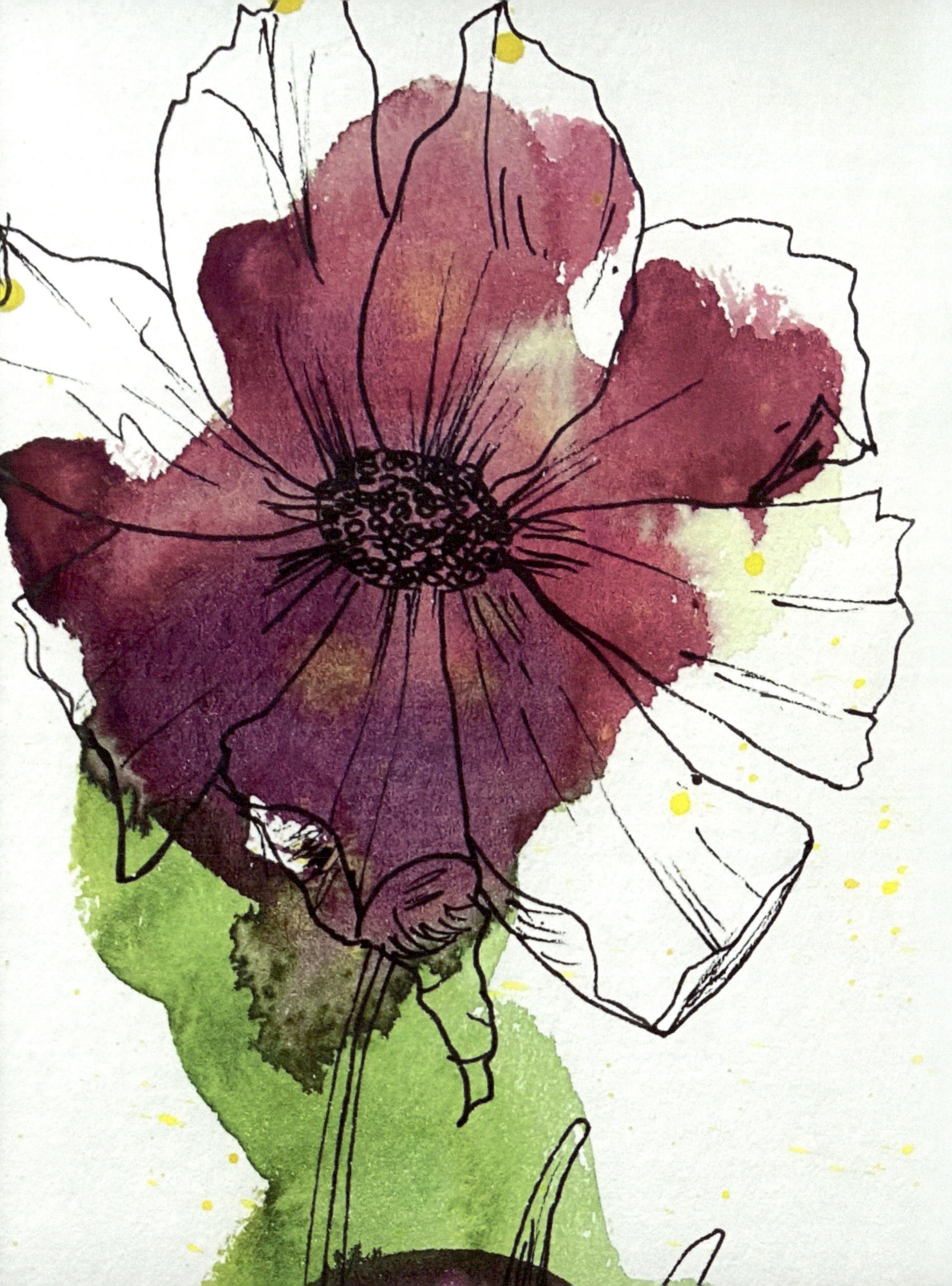

Keeping Safe

This morning
I have tears
in my throat
and heavy eyes

Enveloped
by the darkness
and winter wind
keeping safe

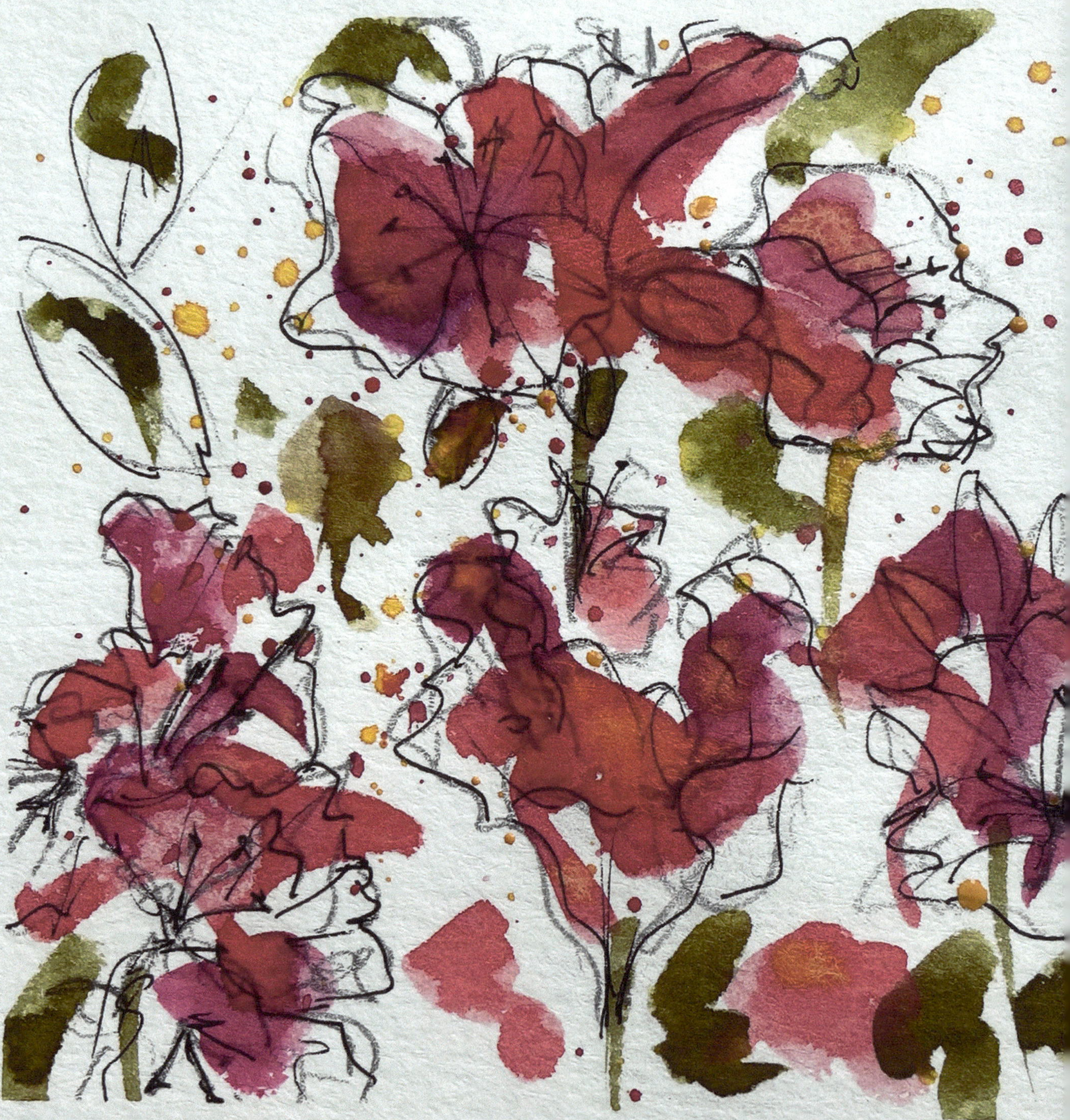

Responsibility

Responsibility
is a welcome burden
to those who find there
food for hungry spaces
and hide themselves
within
bathing in
small vanities
of self-importance

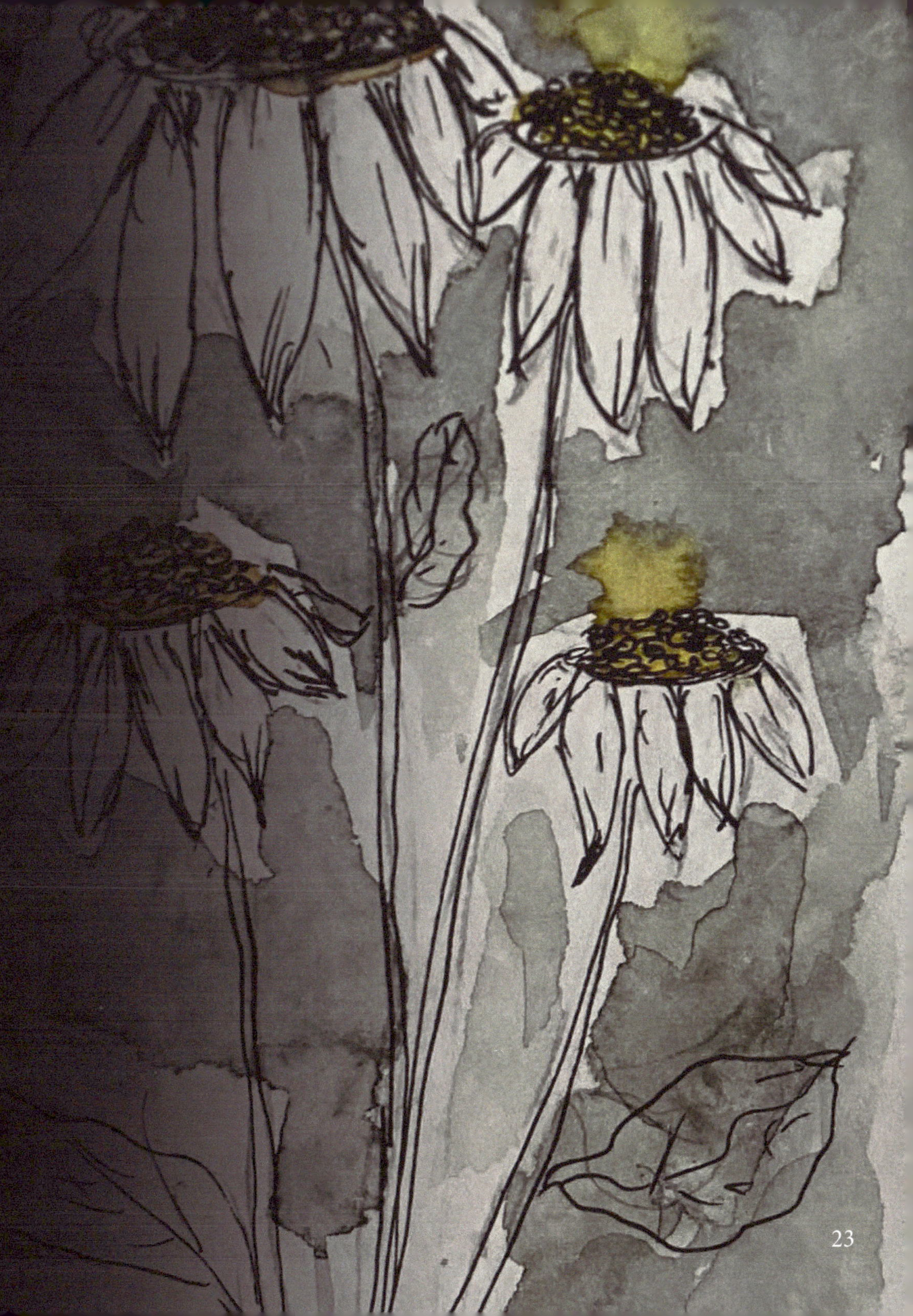

Black

Umbrellas like devil canopies
walls houses roads
are black
leaves like cornflakes soaked in
milk too long
Lie in oily pools
black boots march
with even steps
the good
cry out for help

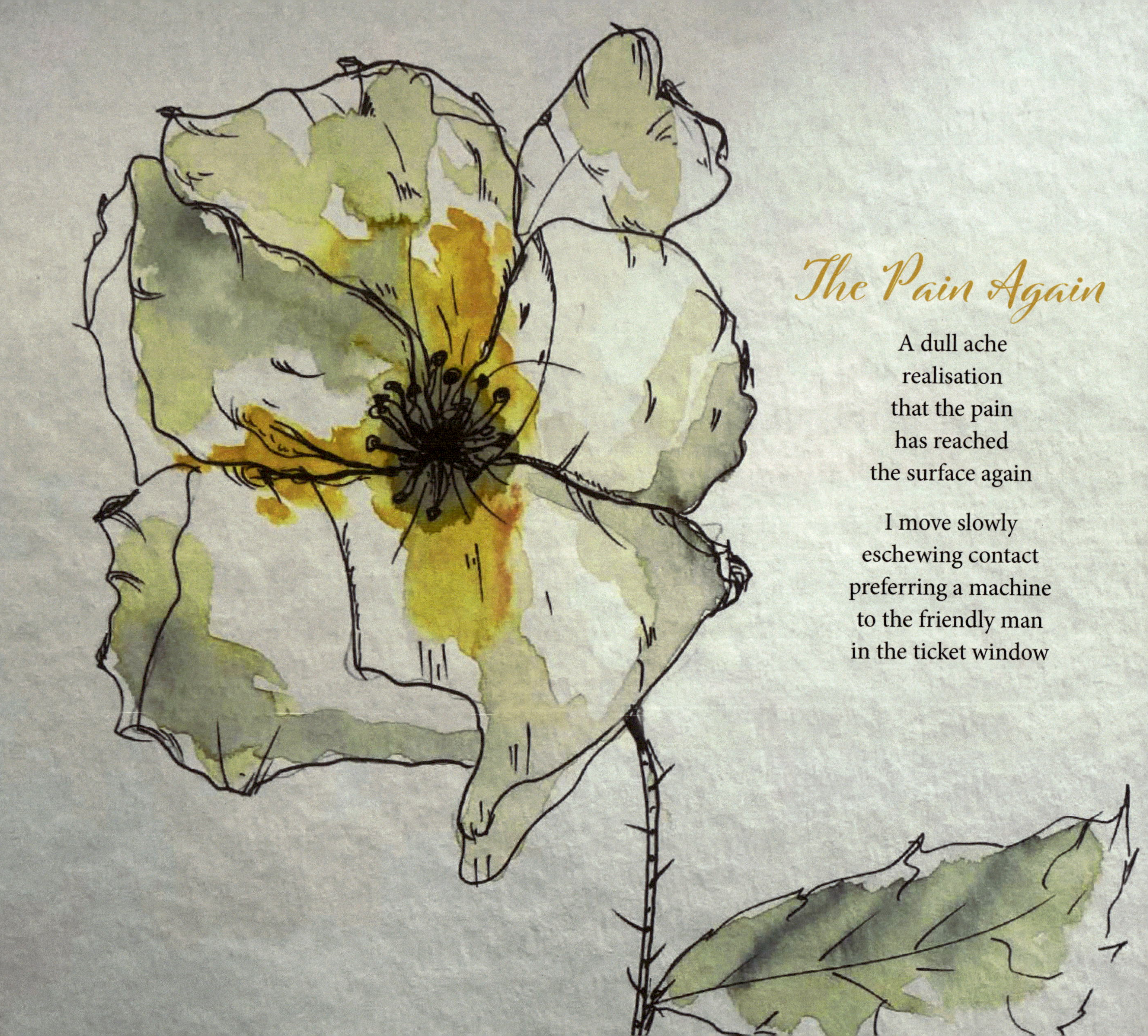

The Pain Again

A dull ache
realisation
that the pain
has reached
the surface again

I move slowly
eschewing contact
preferring a machine
to the friendly man
in the ticket window

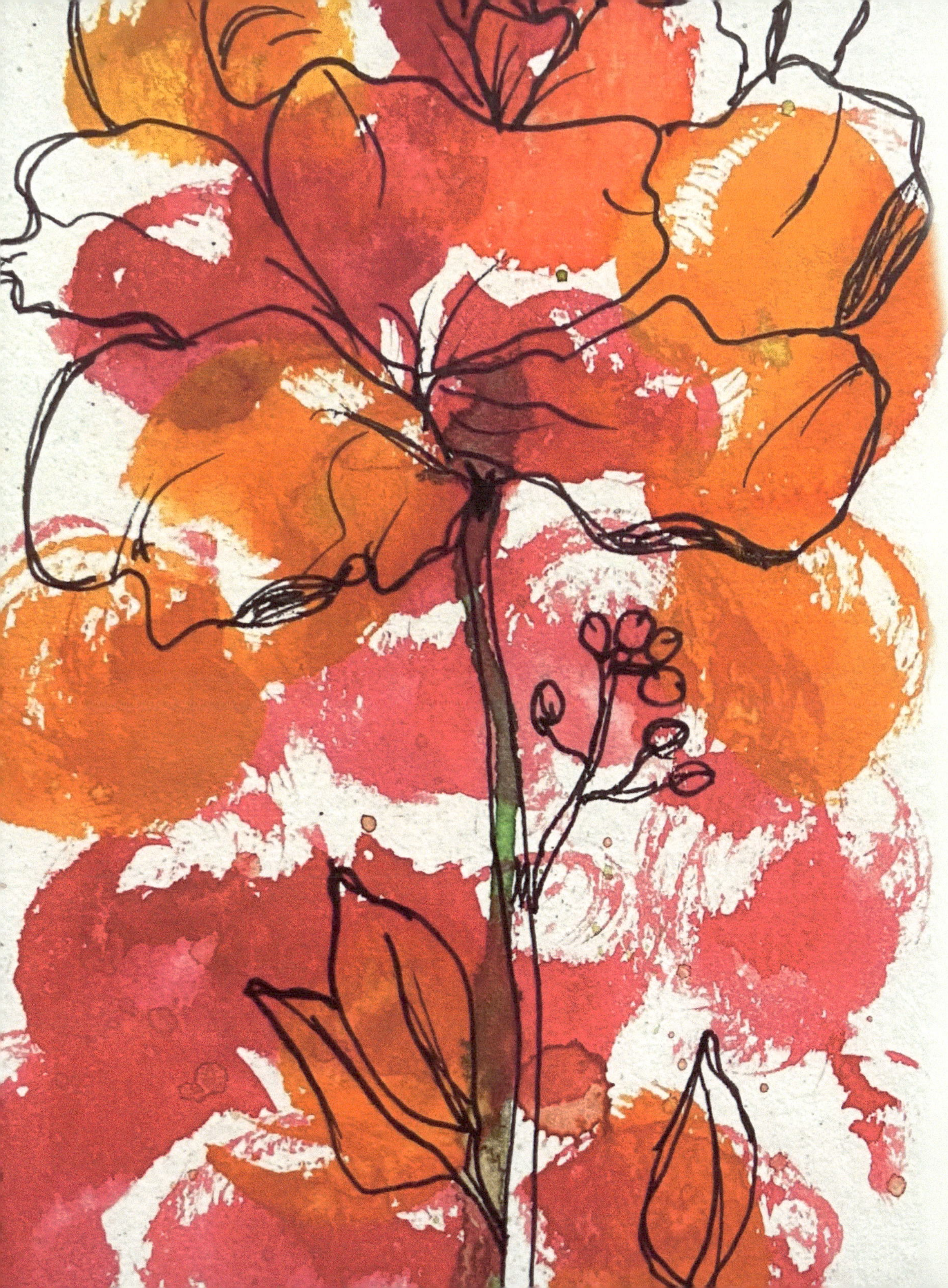

My Smiling Heart

This morning
a new experience
an all-over body-smile

My heart has carried
me for so long
now I am learning
to treasure
and caress it

A new life
is opening
for me
from the inside out
I must follow
this call

Emergence

Waiting feels
different
now

What may
arise
is not
mine

Yet asks
to be shared

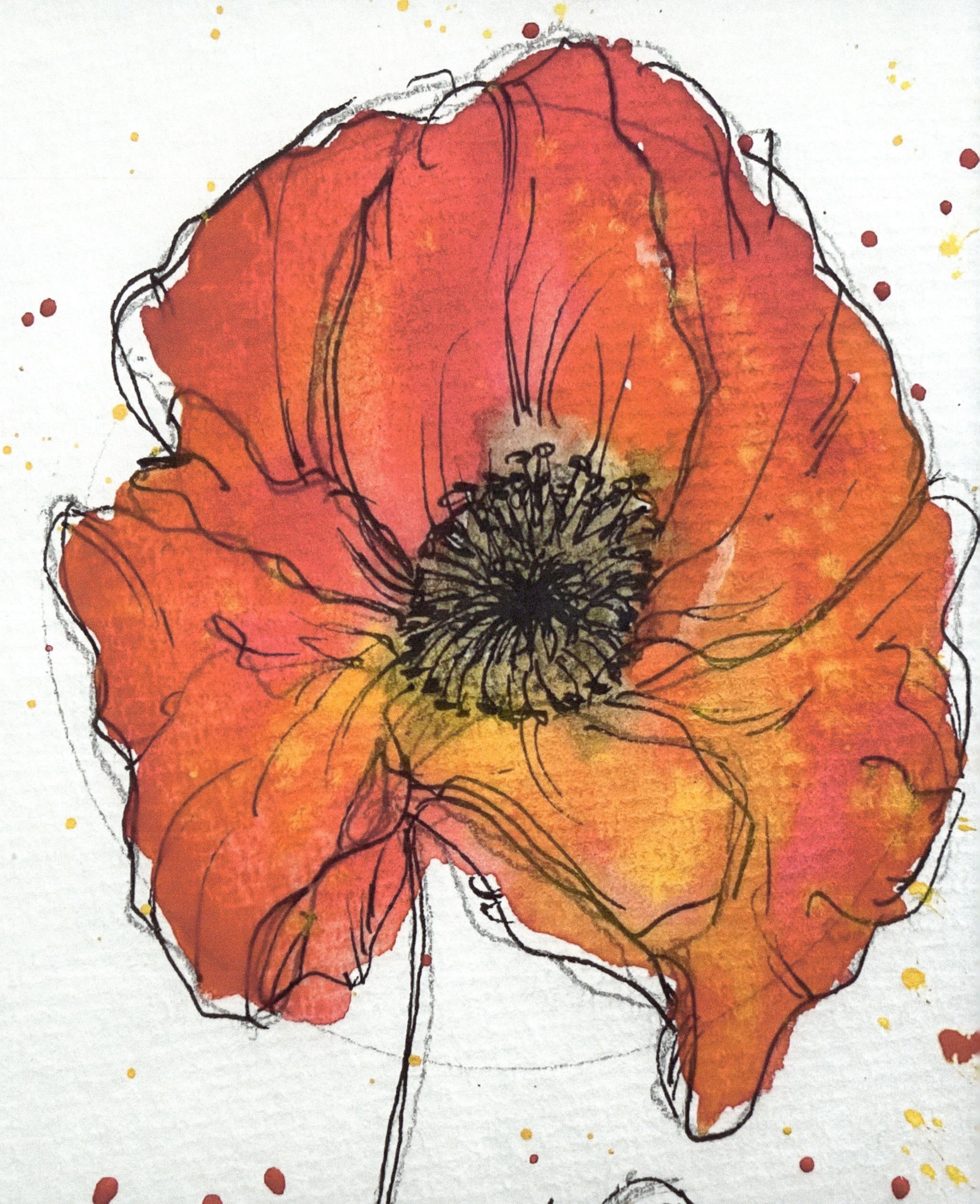

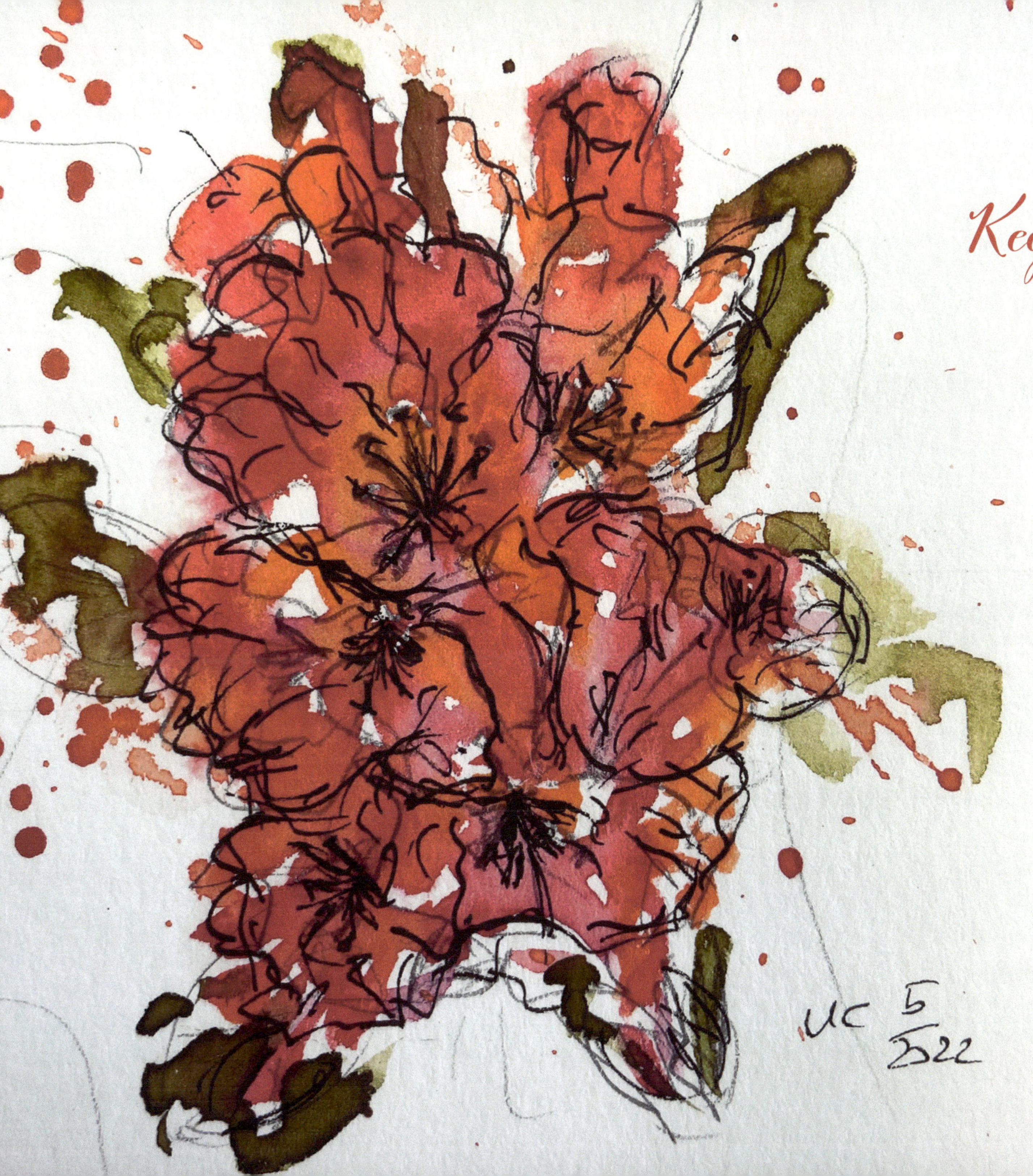

Keep Breathing

Kneading
pushing rolling
the breath
focus
on the breath
loosen
loosen now
let go
you are alive
breathe ha!
out-breath
focus
on the breath
no fear
let it go

Precious Time

Minutes hours
with the one
I love

Priceless
to have
no agenda
no tasks
just being
together

History
all around
to savour

Passions
to renew

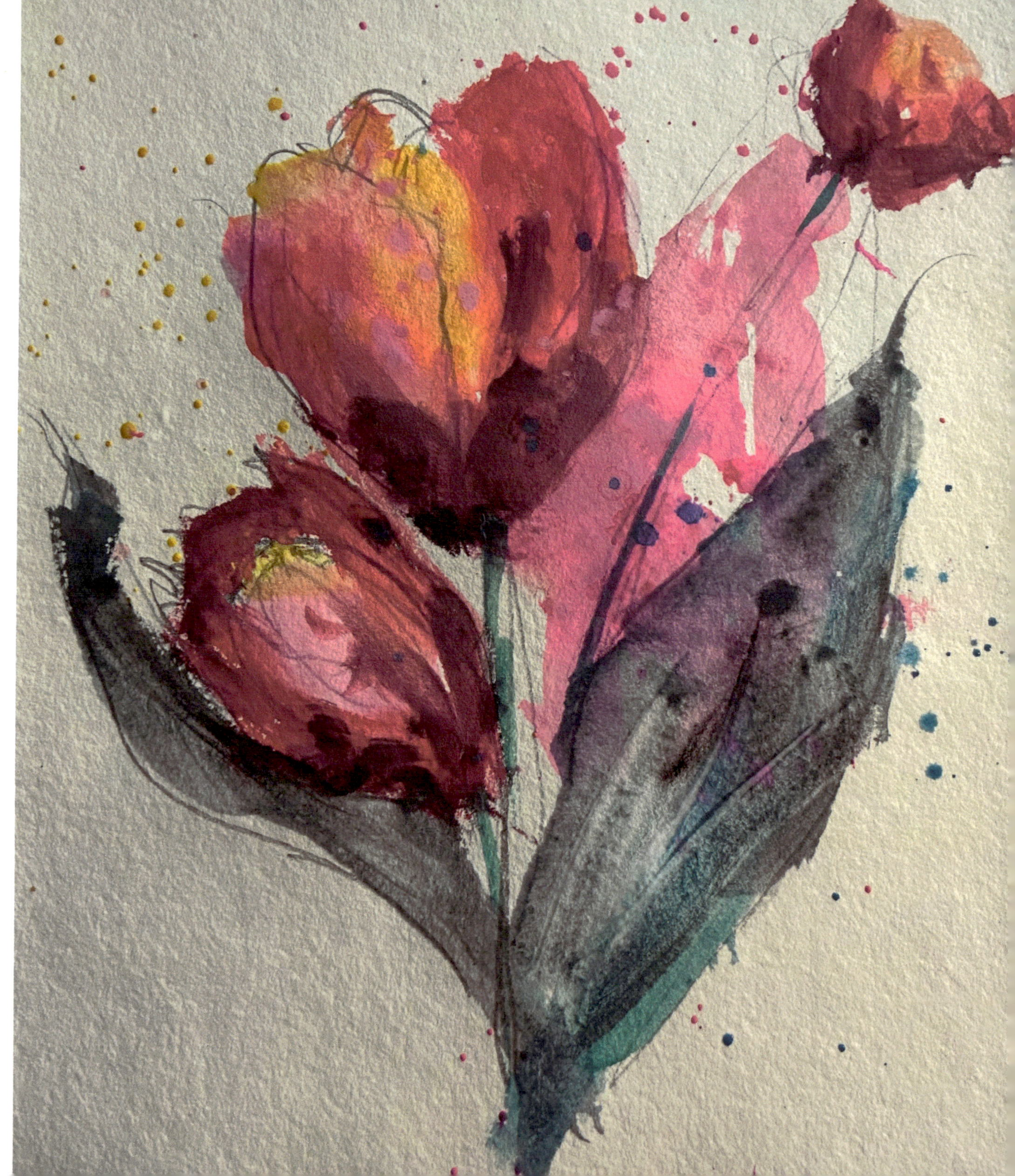

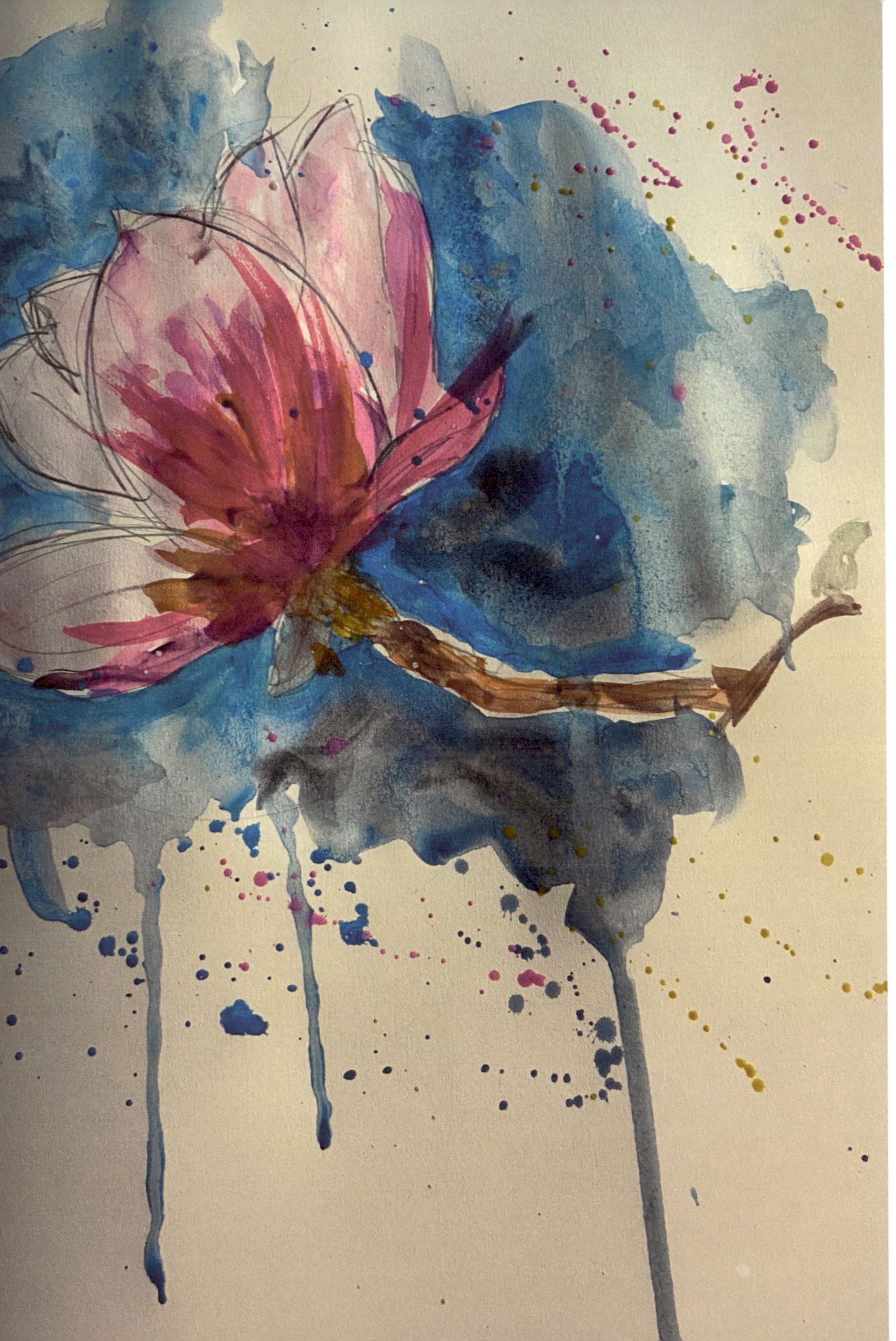

My Lockdown Gifts

I shyly admit
to receiving
precious gifts
from lockdown

Space for reflection
control of my day

Opportunities arise
from close living
to receive
important feedback
from those I love

Practises emerge
in this fertile space
restraint and
personal containment
let the heart open

New understandings
abound on
transition
and change
as I work
on endings
while imagining
beginnings

Poems

ILLUSTRATED WITH PHOTOS

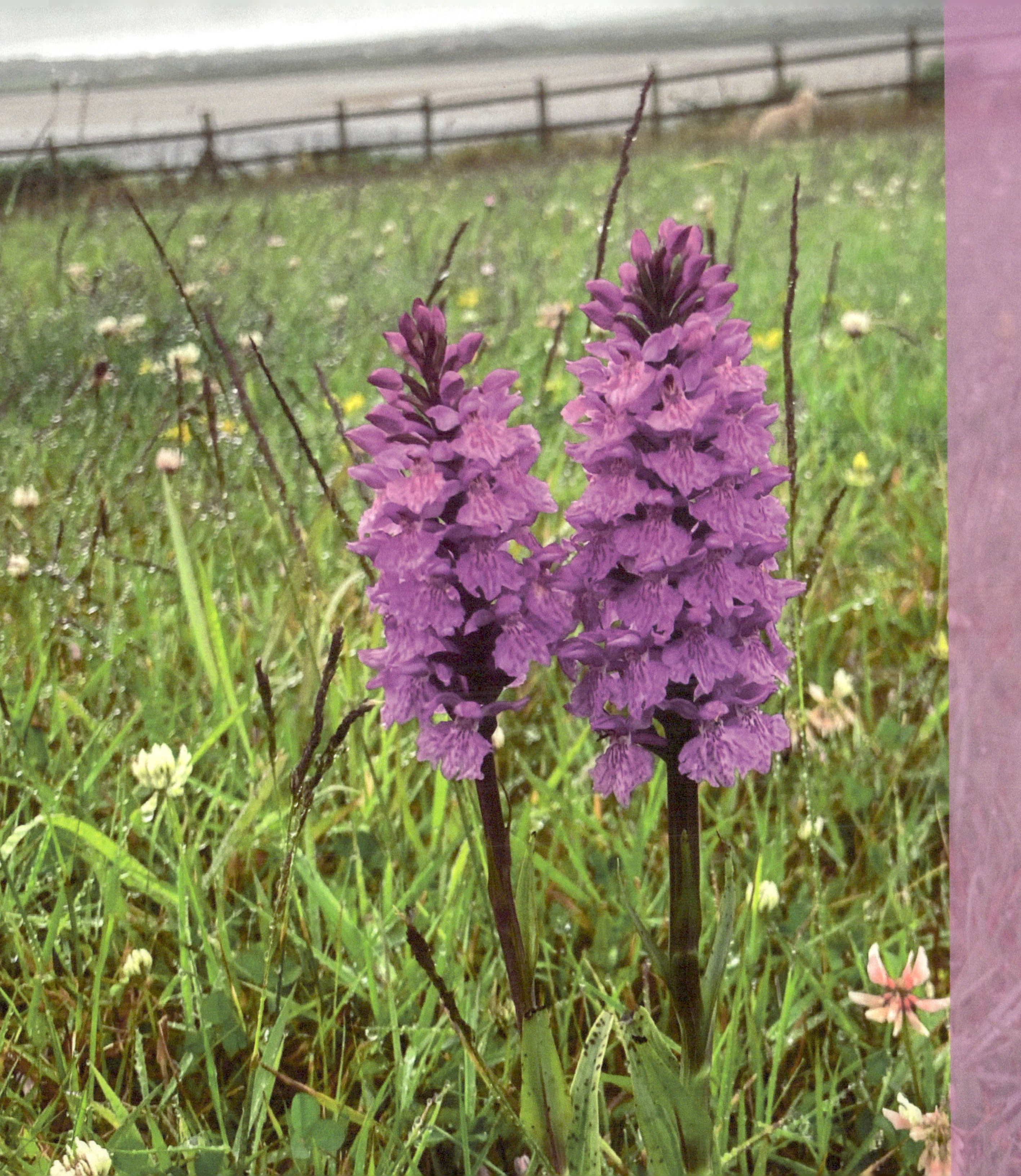

Deep Joy

I am
a Poet
a vessel
for words
to stumble
through and from

Since
my teens
my poems
have provided
signposts to
my life
and its unfolding

Today
I am bathed in
so many gifts
and healings
that pain and loss
have been
moulded into
deep joy

An Introvert's Prayer

Grant me spaces
between my encounters
enough me-time
to recover

Lead me to
wild places
where light and water
dance

May my being
be valued
as much as
my doing

Healer

I am
a healer
please help
yourself
to the gifts
we all share
grace mercy
forgiveness gentleness
and love

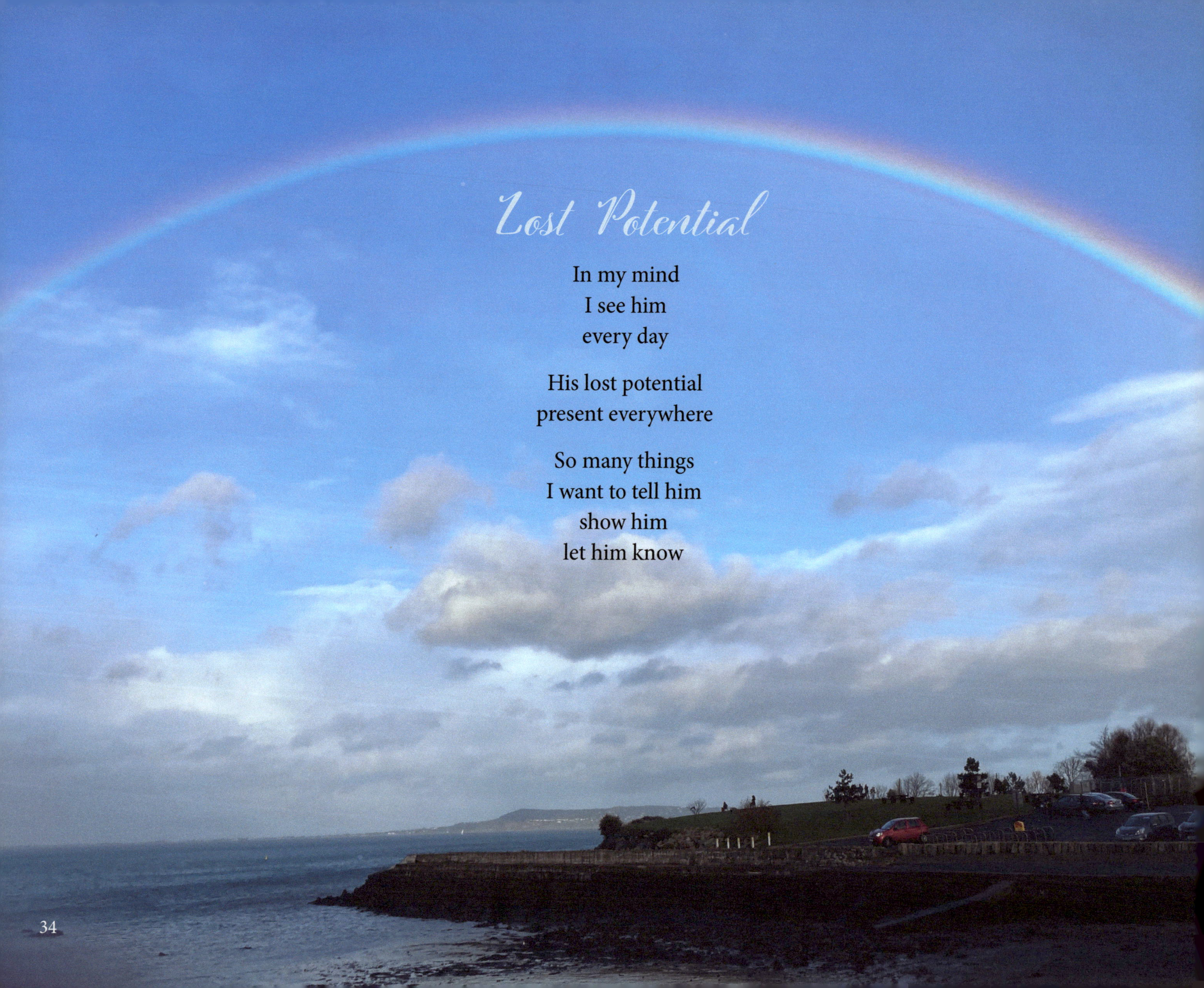
Lost Potential

In my mind
I see him
every day

His lost potential
present everywhere

So many things
I want to tell him
show him
let him know

34

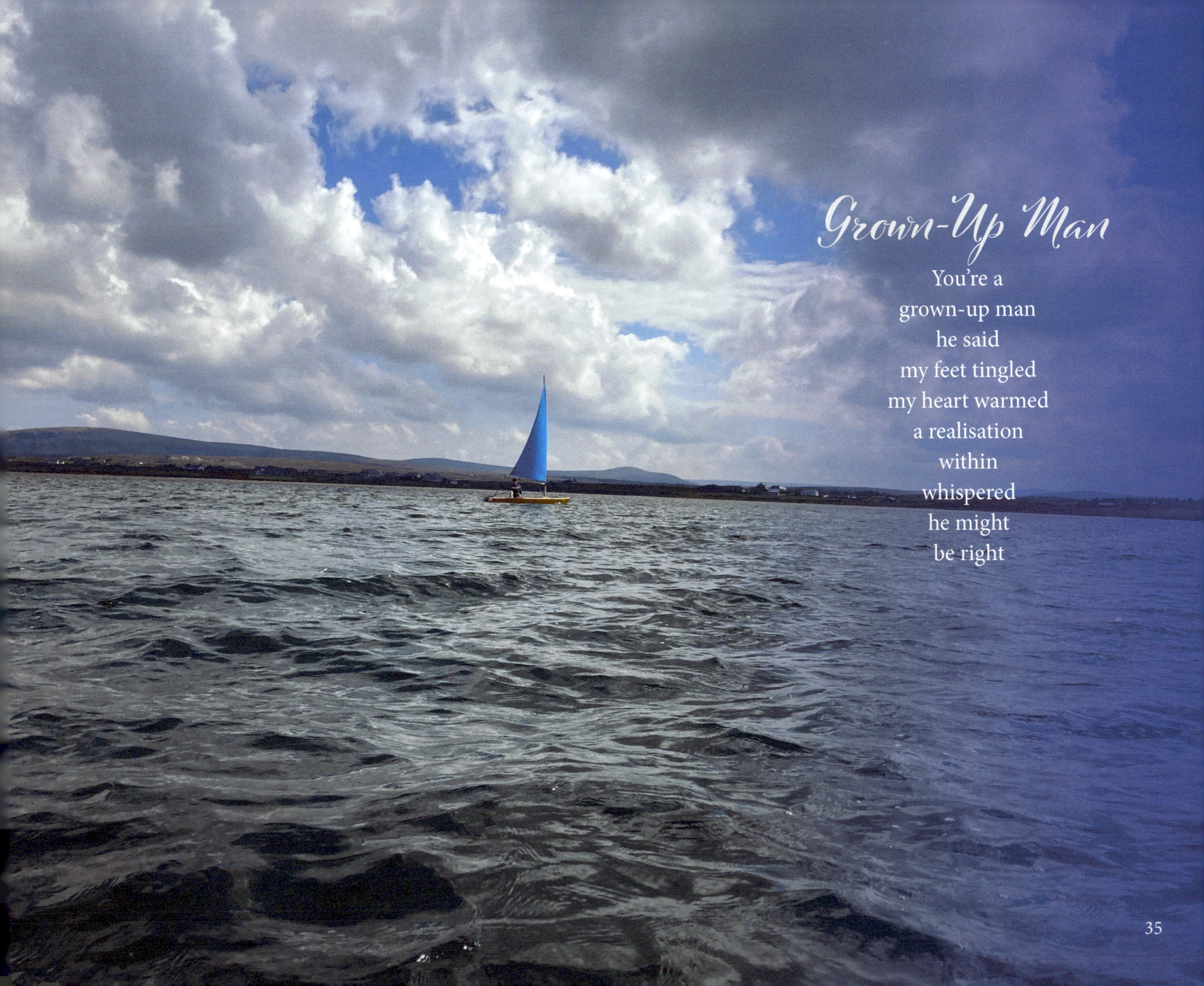

Grown-Up Man

You're a
grown-up man
he said
my feet tingled
my heart warmed
a realisation
within
whispered
he might
be right

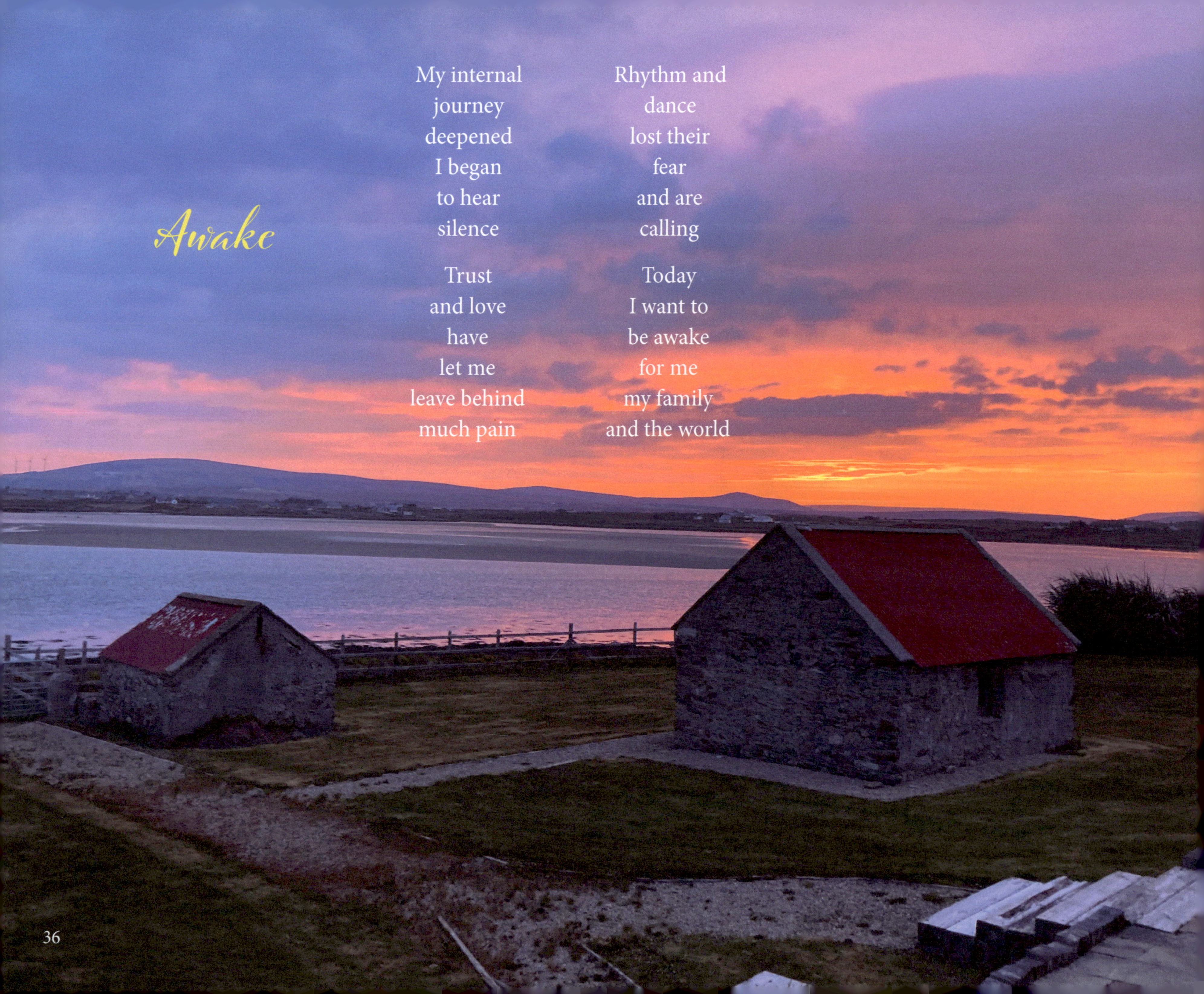

Awake

My internal
journey
deepened
I began
to hear
silence

Trust
and love
have
let me
leave behind
much pain

Rhythm and
dance
lost their
fear
and are
calling

Today
I want to
be awake
for me
my family
and the world

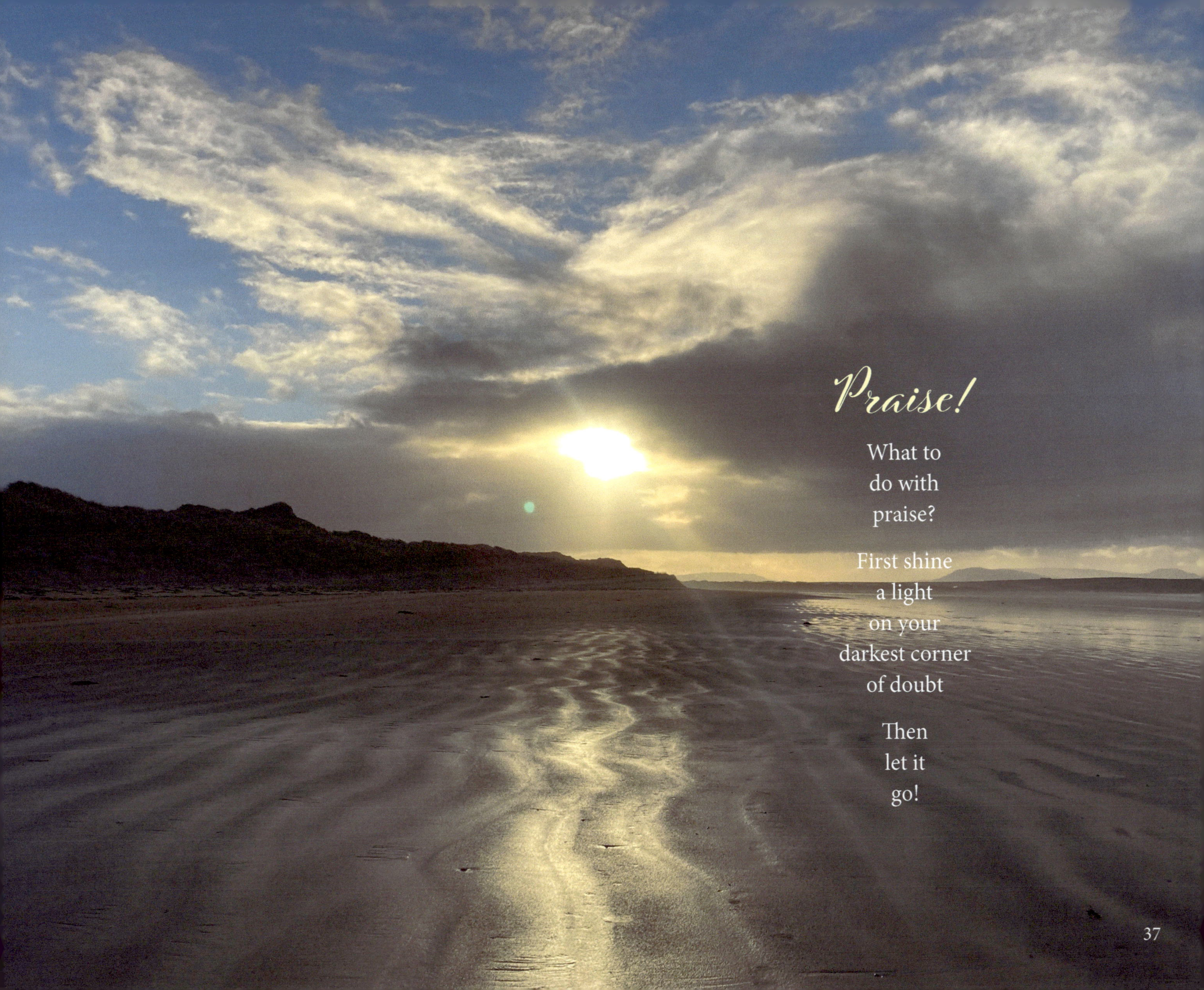

Praise!

What to
do with
praise?

First shine
a light
on your
darkest corner
of doubt

Then
let it
go!

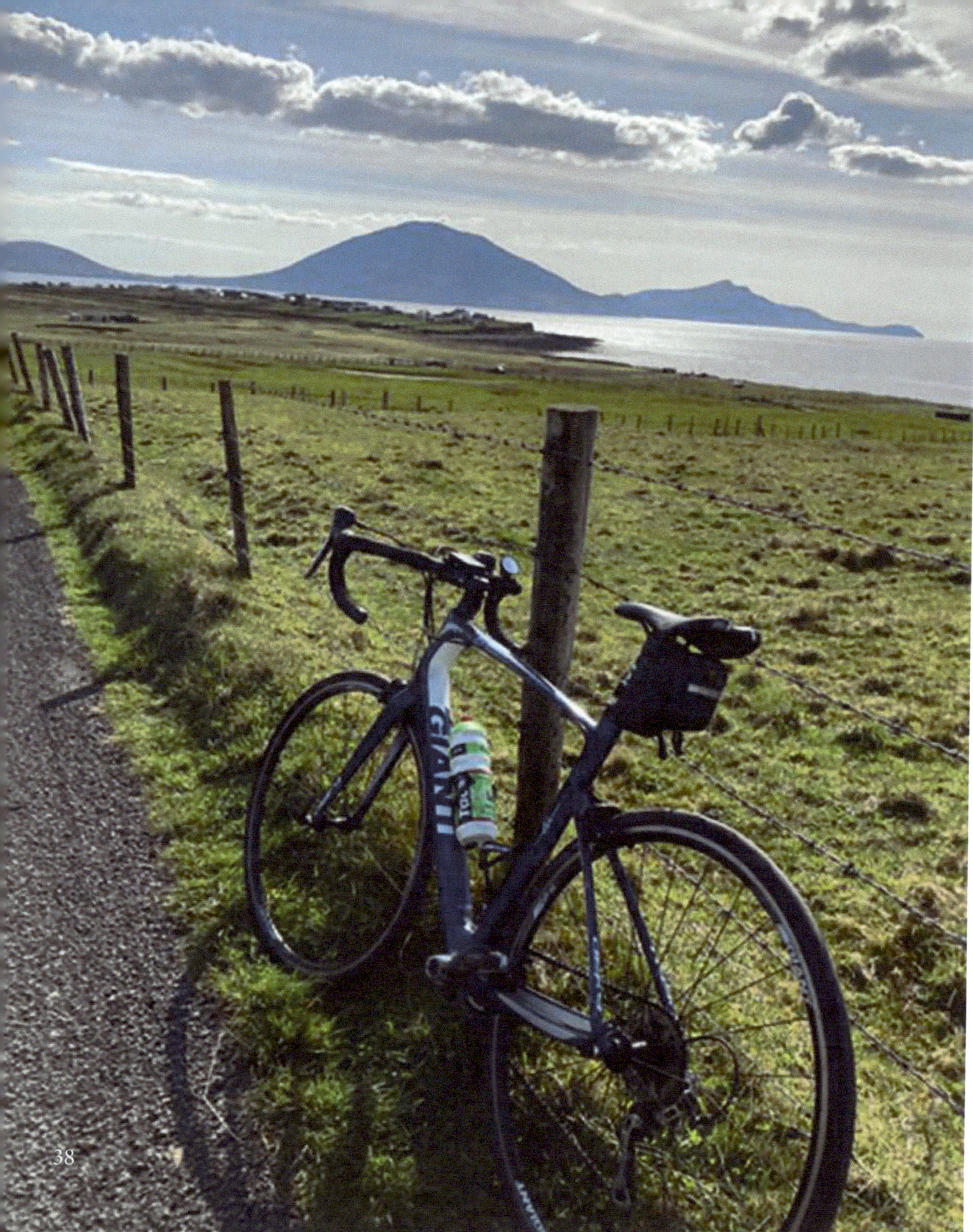

A Moment

On my bike
on the sea-road
to Doohoma
A bullfinch
catches my eye

As my thoughts
evaporate
I enter fully
into this moment
for the first time

With my attention caught
birdsong all around
keeps me in the moment
like the Myna Birds
In Huxley's 'Island'

I stop and lie
facing Achill Island
on the sloping roadside
and write these lines

The Call

I am being called
by something that
won't leave
me at peace

It is the call of
the dying planet
our home

Sometimes
it is so strong
It overwhelms me

But now
I must be still
And listen

Ask my heart
what is
the message
For me?

What must
I do?

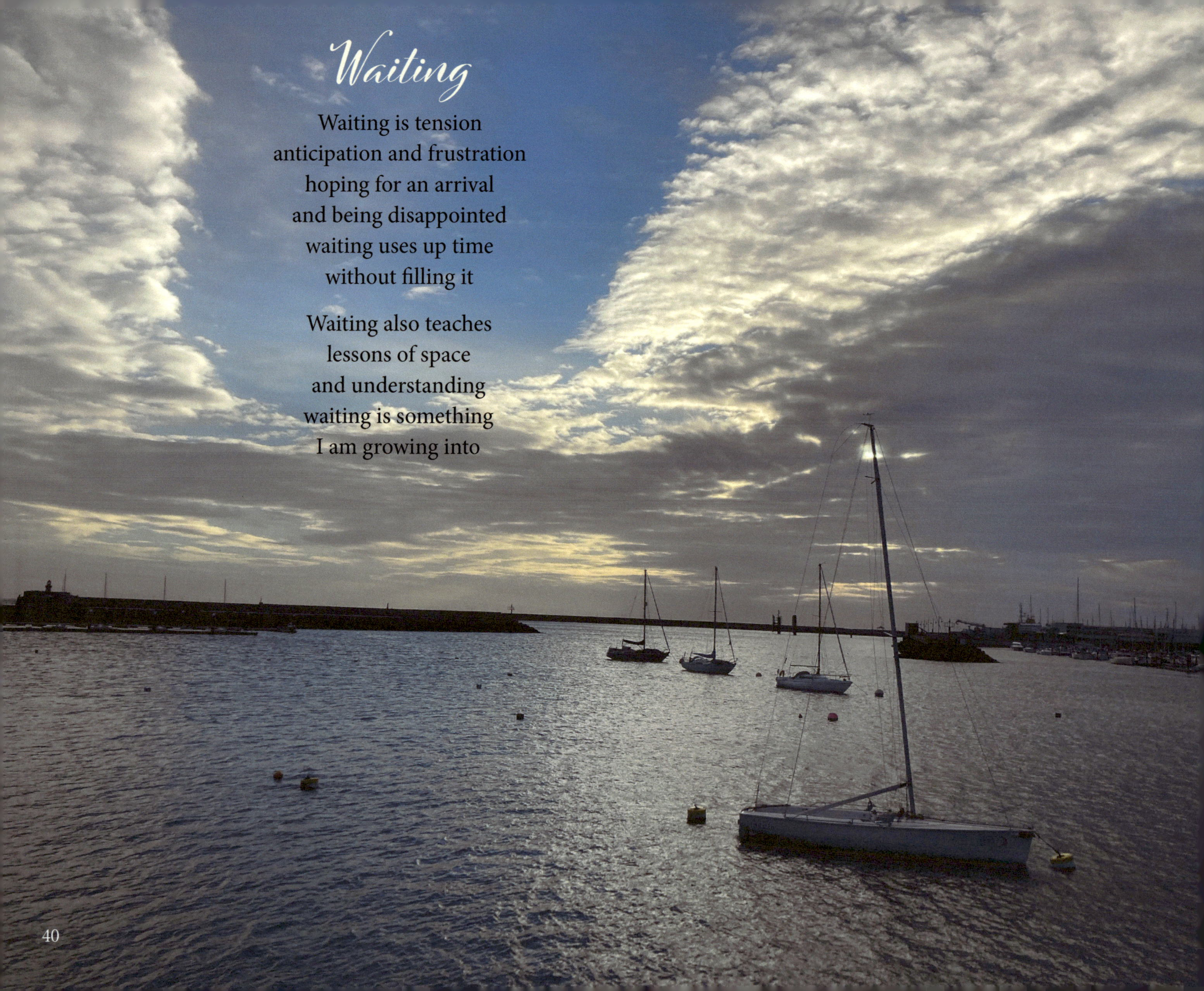

Waiting

Waiting is tension
anticipation and frustration
hoping for an arrival
and being disappointed
waiting uses up time
without filling it

Waiting also teaches
lessons of space
and understanding
waiting is something
I am growing into

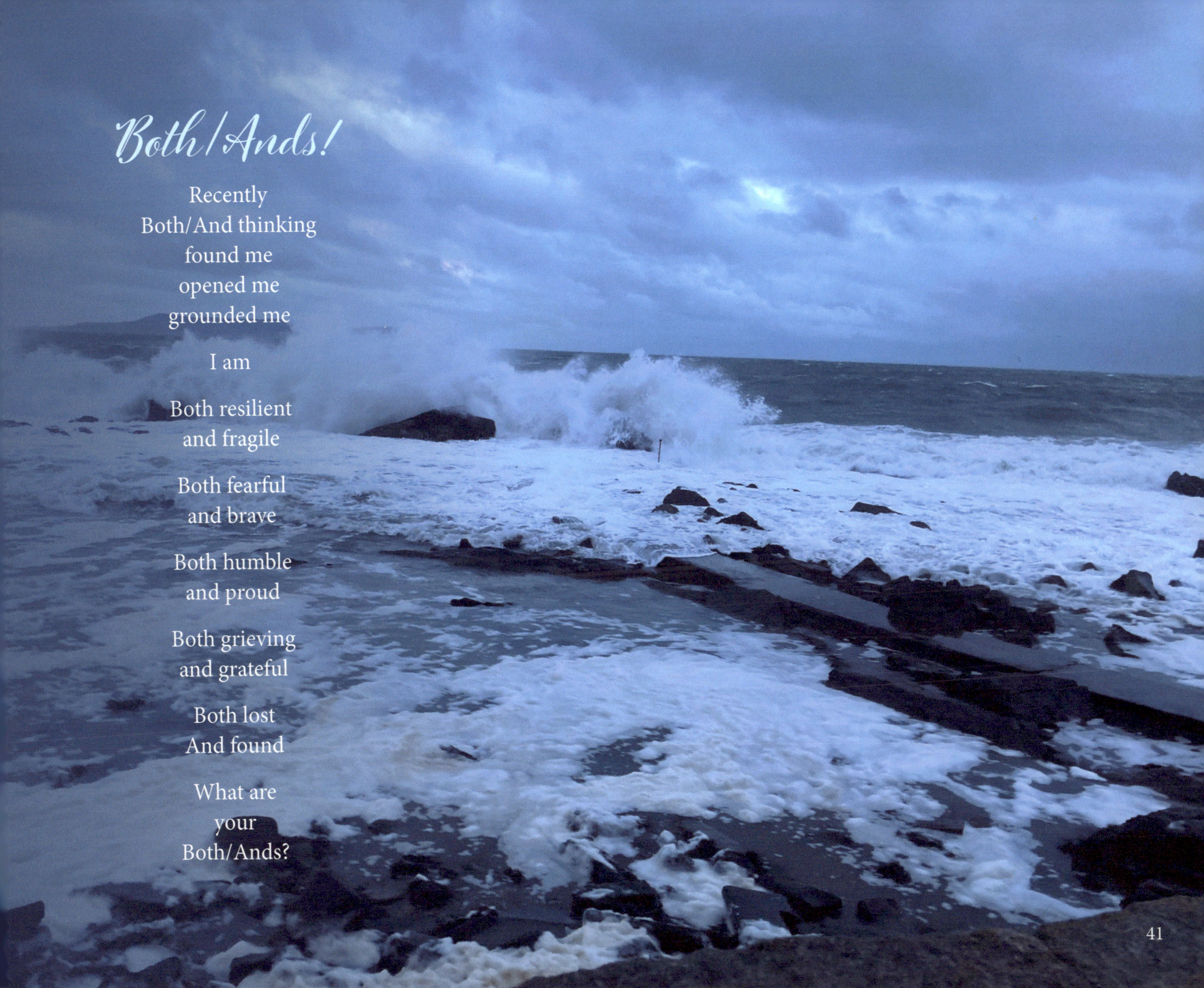

Both/Ands!

Recently
Both/And thinking
found me
opened me
grounded me

I am

Both resilient
and fragile

Both fearful
and brave

Both humble
and proud

Both grieving
and grateful

Both lost
And found

What are
your
Both/Ands?

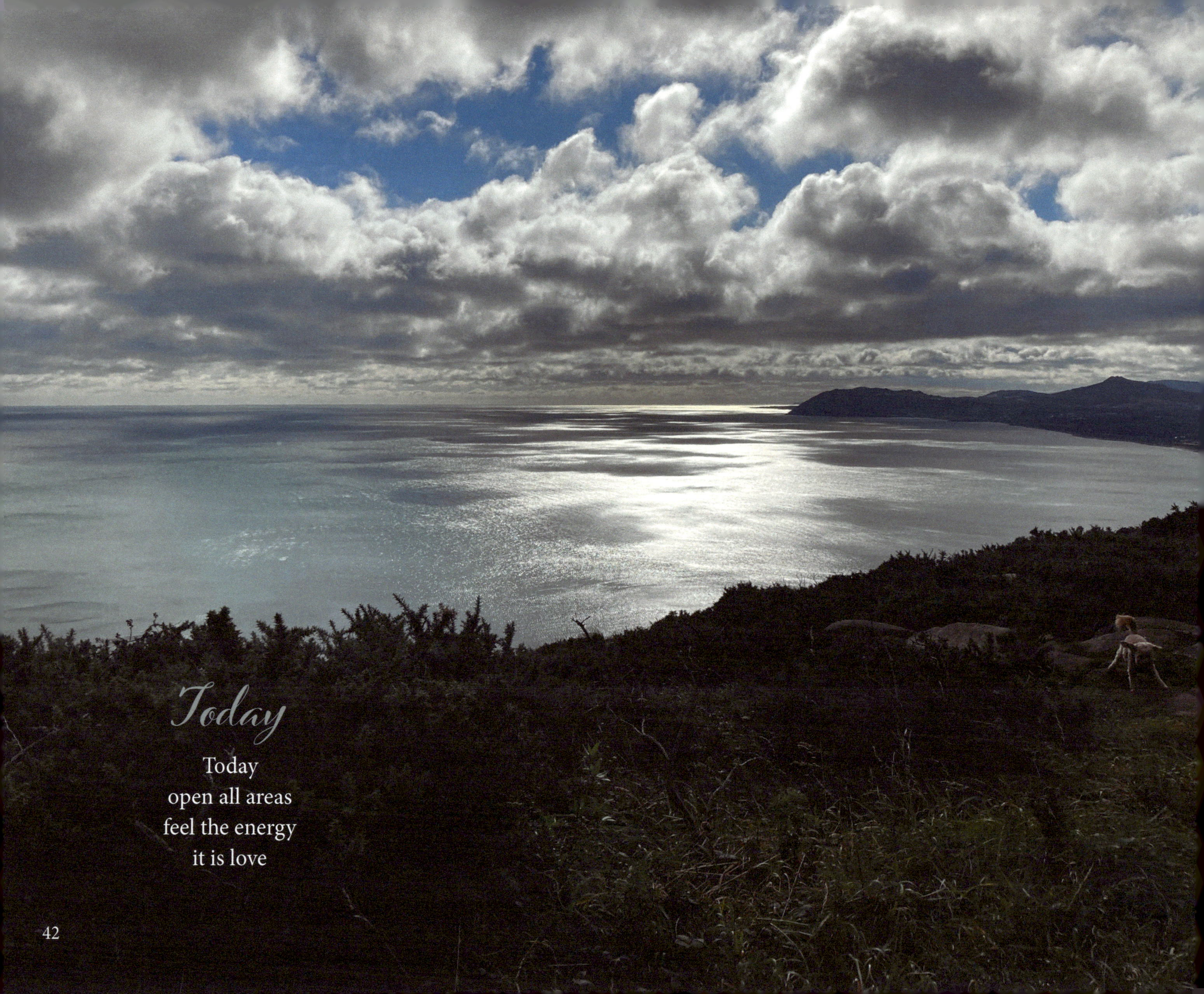
Today

Today
open all areas
feel the energy
it is love

Overload

This morning
I am fragile
tearful
feeling
overwhelmed

Battered
by the week
little space
always on
no distance
fractured boundaries

Then I see
the moon
feel its
healing pull

A flight of birds
lift me
and ease
my pain

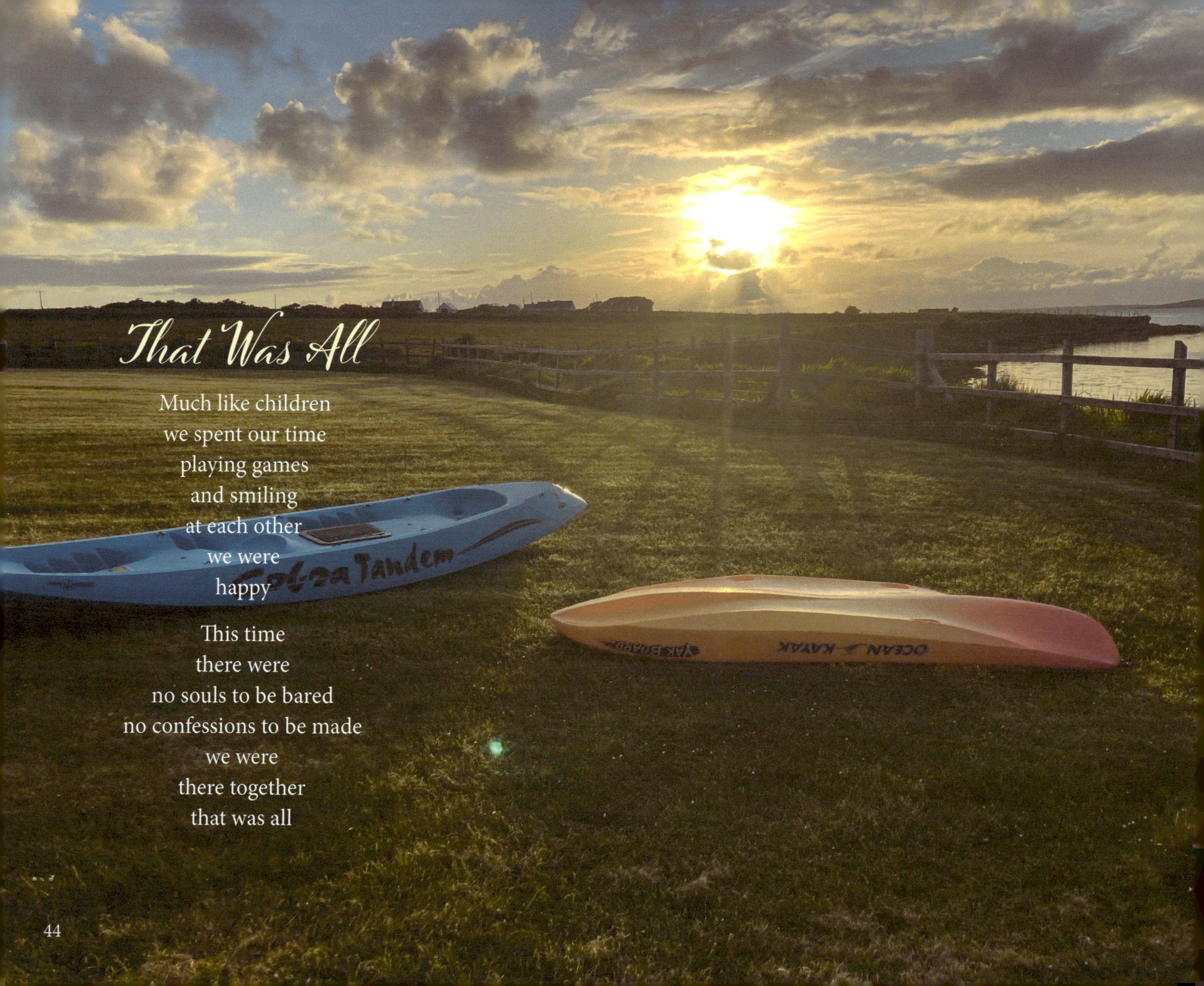

That Was All

Much like children
we spent our time
playing games
and smiling
at each other
we were
happy

This time
there were
no souls to be bared
no confessions to be made
we were
there together
that was all

Lessons

The lessons that we learn
are hard and real
those who are open
are constantly surprised

Discipline brings freedom
restraint fulfilment

The more we let go
the more we have

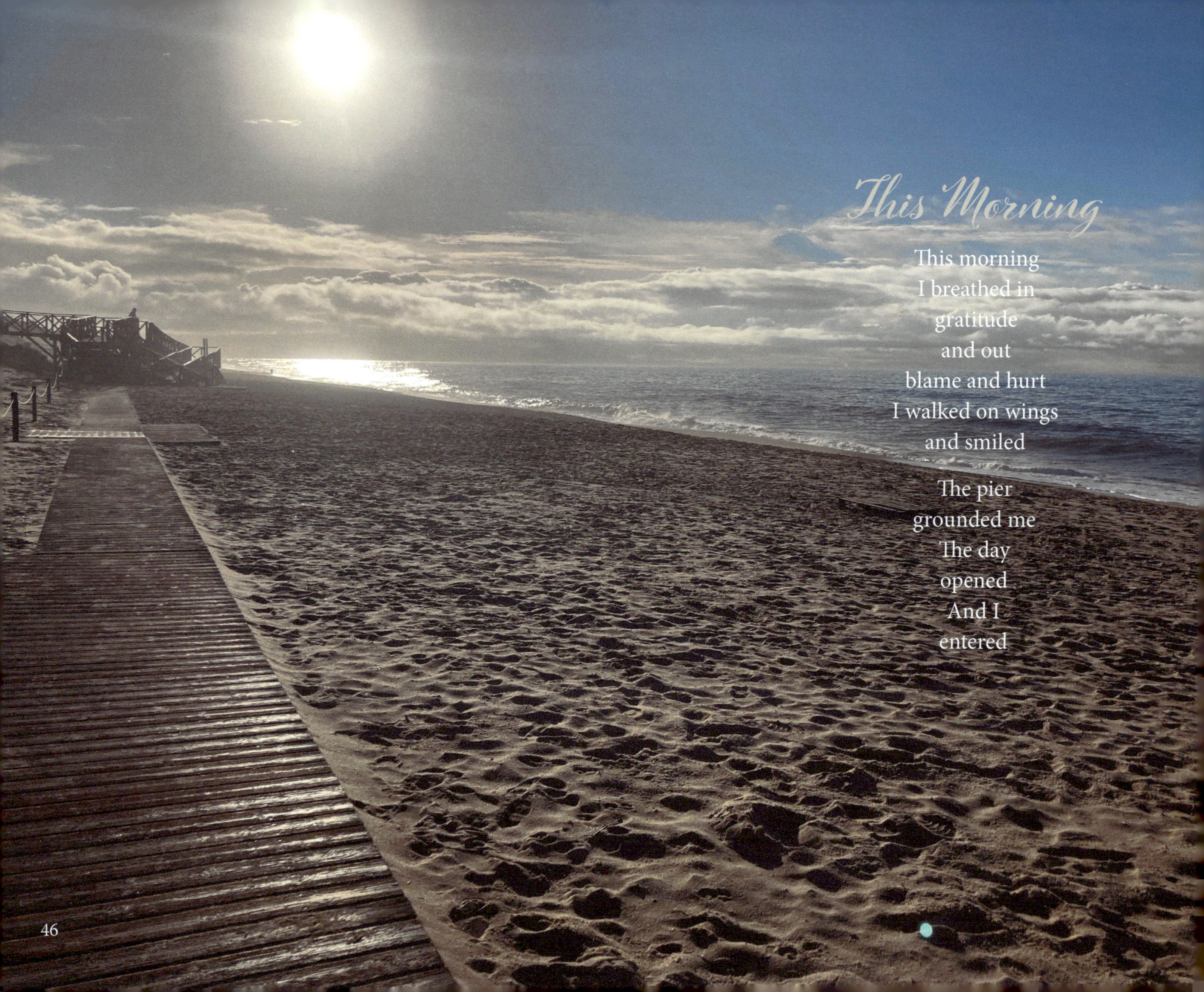

This Morning

This morning
I breathed in
gratitude
and out
blame and hurt
I walked on wings
and smiled

The pier
grounded me
The day
opened
And I
entered

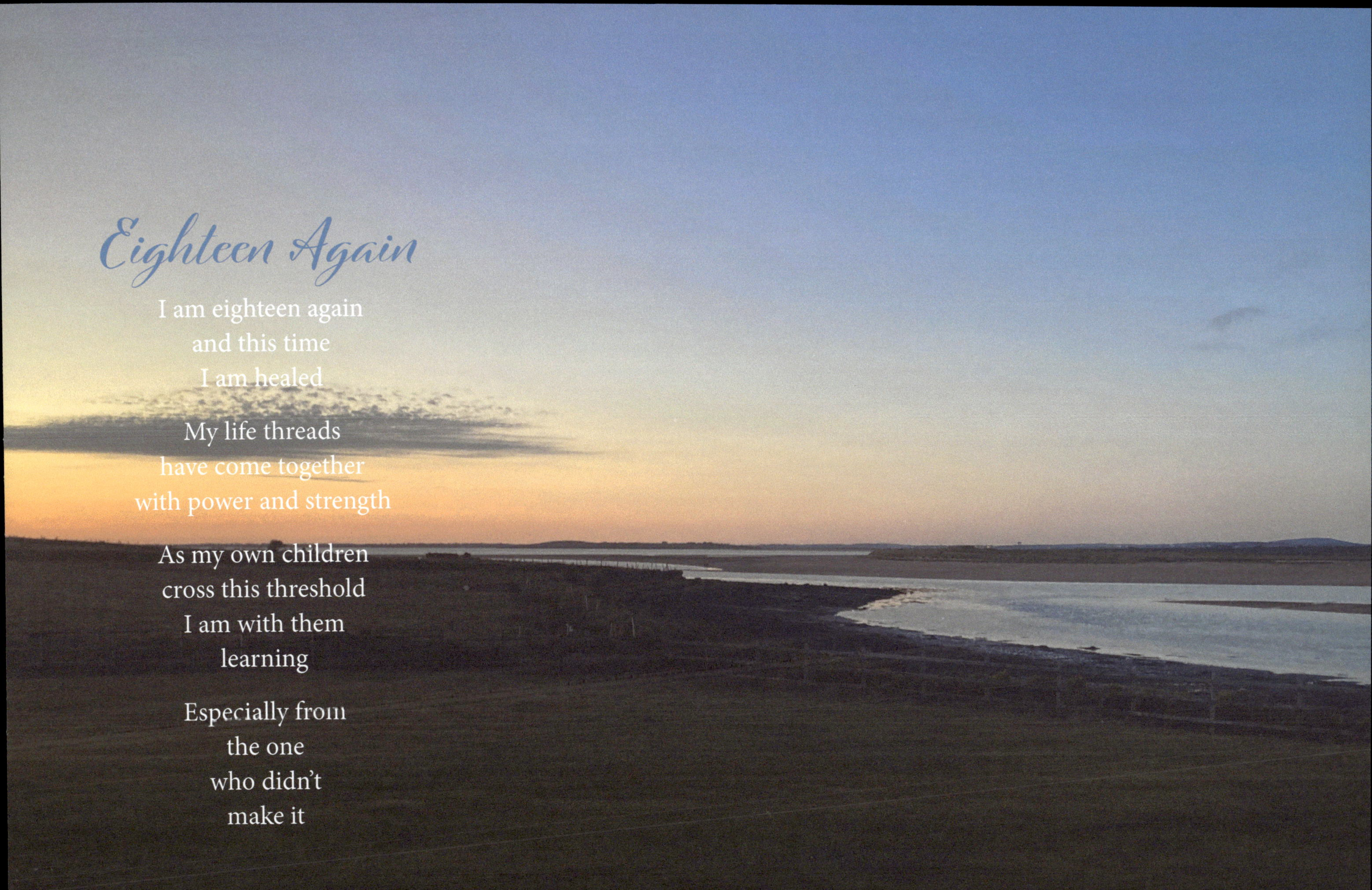

Eighteen Again

I am eighteen again
and this time
I am healed

My life threads
have come together
with power and strength

As my own children
cross this threshold
I am with them
learning

Especially from
the one
who didn't
make it

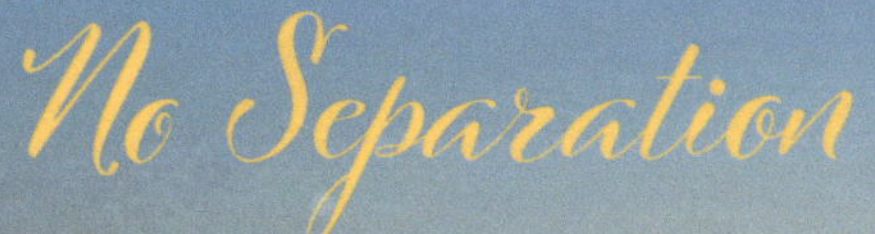

No Separation

I don't know
anymore
where I start
and finish

I seem
to be a part
of everything
and everything
seems to be
a part of me

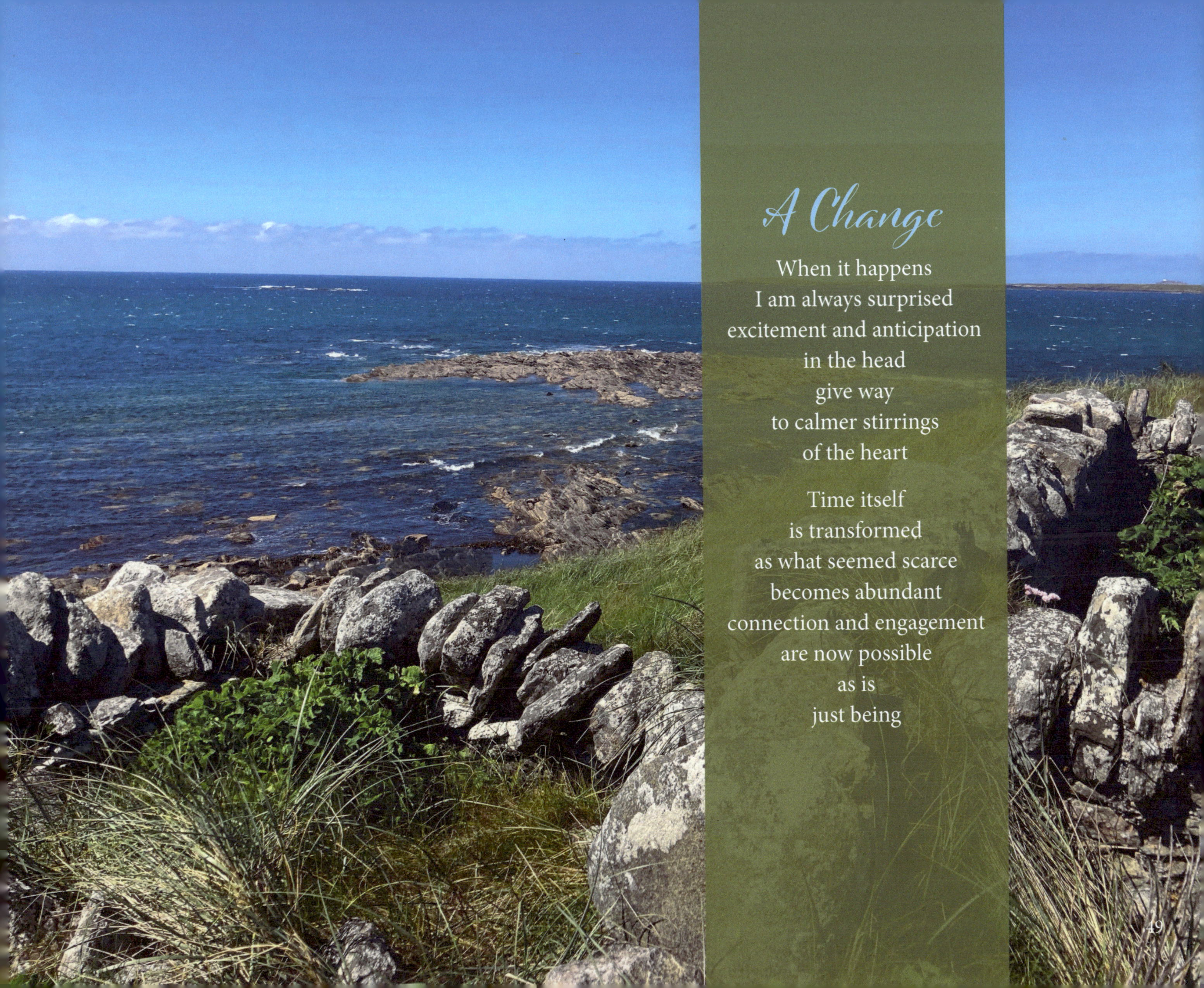

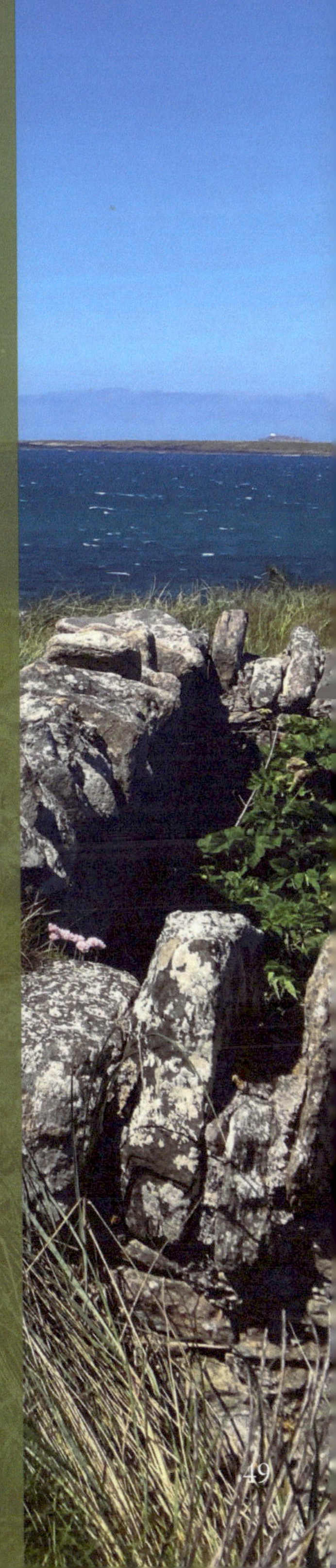

A Change

When it happens
I am always surprised
excitement and anticipation
in the head
give way
to calmer stirrings
of the heart

Time itself
is transformed
as what seemed scarce
becomes abundant
connection and engagement
are now possible
as is
just being

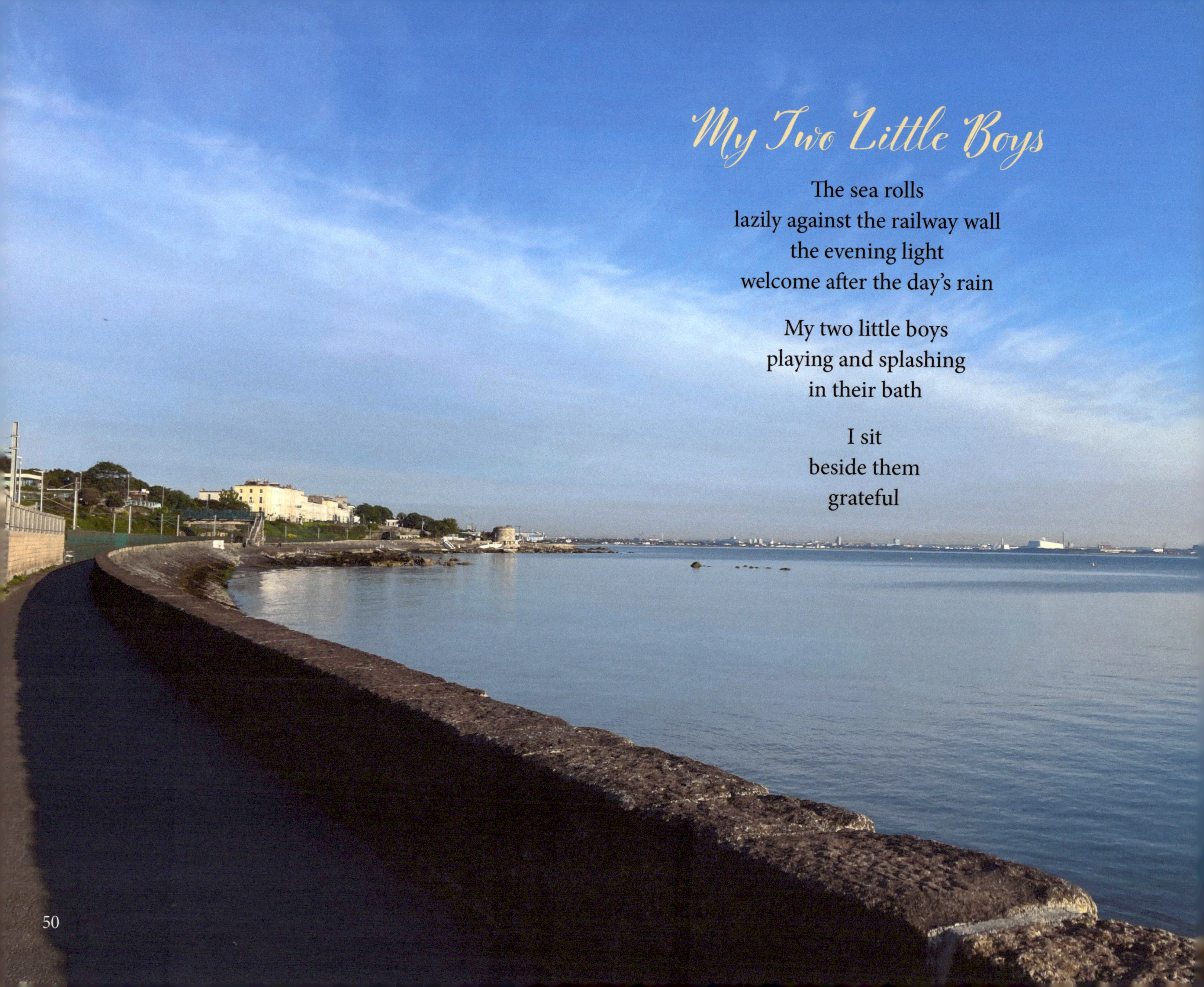

My Two Little Boys

The sea rolls
lazily against the railway wall
the evening light
welcome after the day's rain

My two little boys
playing and splashing
in their bath

I sit
beside them
grateful

I Write Poetry

I write poetry
I said
I do pottery
he said
earlier he said
I have five children
but one has left us
I said
I also have five children
and one has left

We seemed to be
in a bubble together
tears in his eyes
as he spoke about his youngest
who had closed down
he was ten when
his brother died
but now
he is opening again

I listened
held back the urge
to share
that my eldest now
was only ten
when she lost
her brother

We moved on
to wilderness therapy
and the serenity prayer

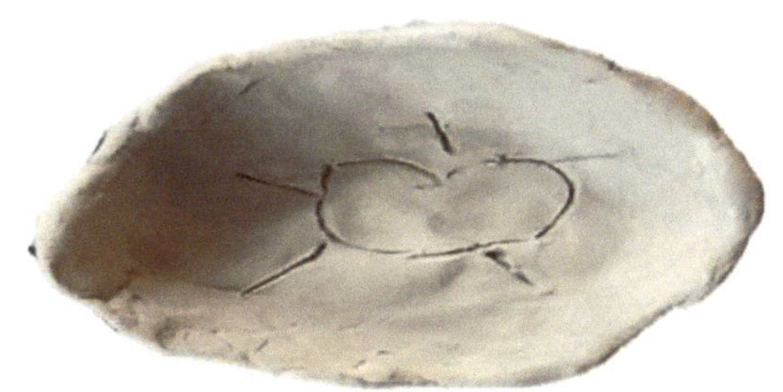

Poems

ILLUSTRATED WITH ECLECTIC ART

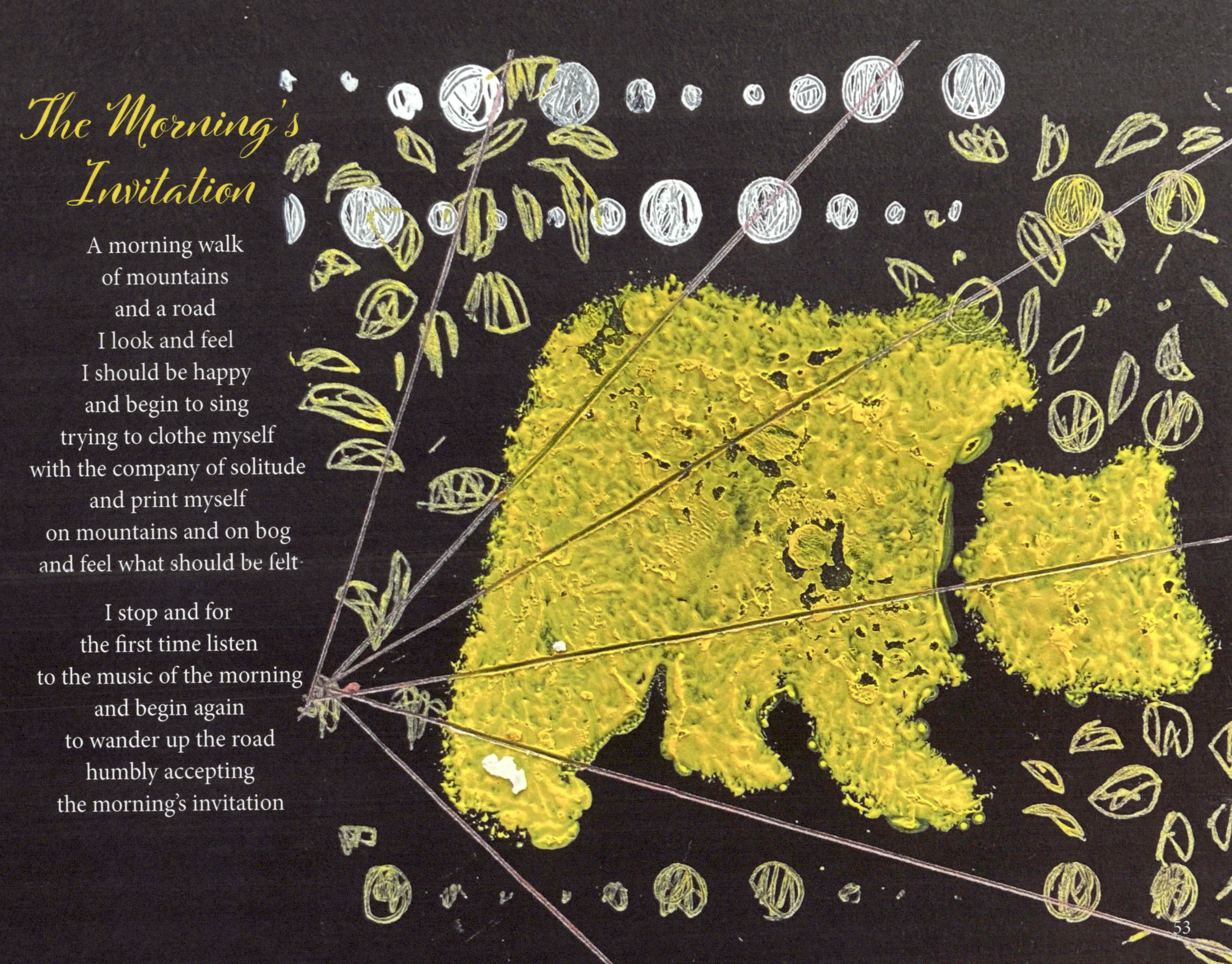

The Morning's Invitation

A morning walk
of mountains
and a road
I look and feel
I should be happy
and begin to sing
trying to clothe myself
with the company of solitude
and print myself
on mountains and on bog
and feel what should be felt

I stop and for
the first time listen
to the music of the morning
and begin again
to wander up the road
humbly accepting
the morning's invitation

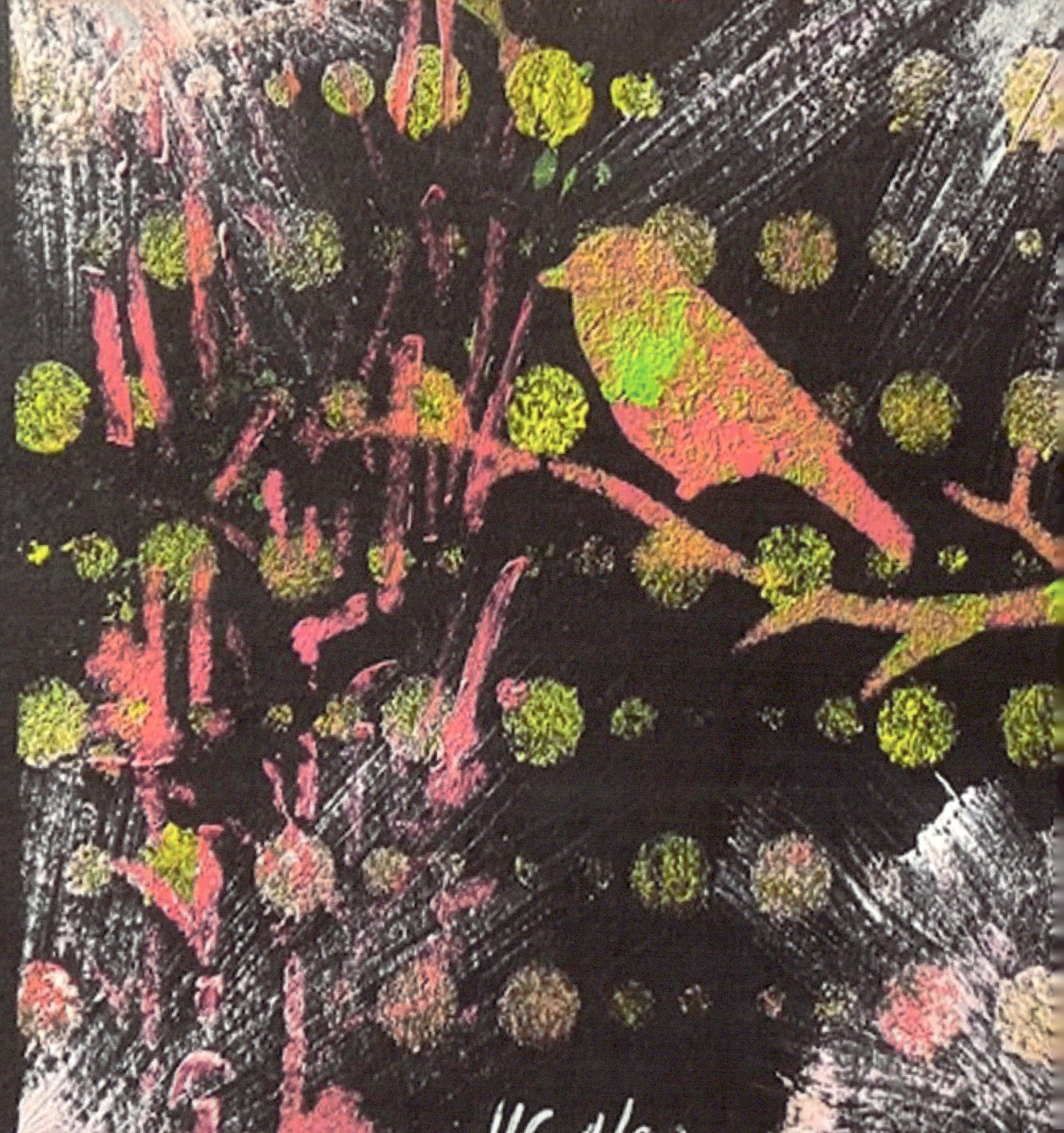

21 01 2022

6am
Friday morning
welcoming the silence
and the dark
I walked
into the garden
and listened
to birdsong

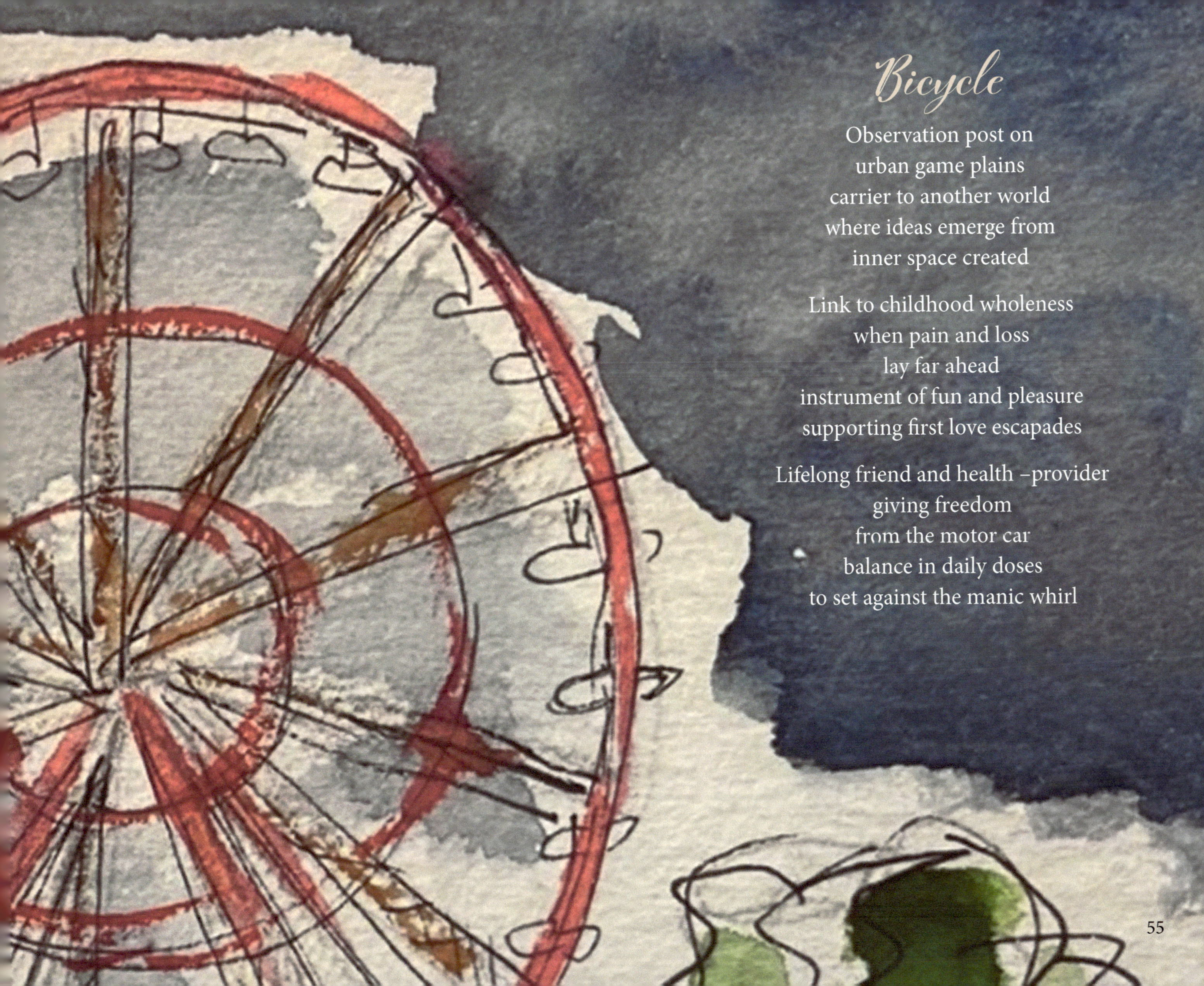

Bicycle

Observation post on
urban game plains
carrier to another world
where ideas emerge from
inner space created

Link to childhood wholeness
when pain and loss
lay far ahead
instrument of fun and pleasure
supporting first love escapades

Lifelong friend and health –provider
giving freedom
from the motor car
balance in daily doses
to set against the manic whirl

Back on the Bike

I had missed
the intense moments

When spinning wheels
occupy my mind

Releasing me
to go
deeper

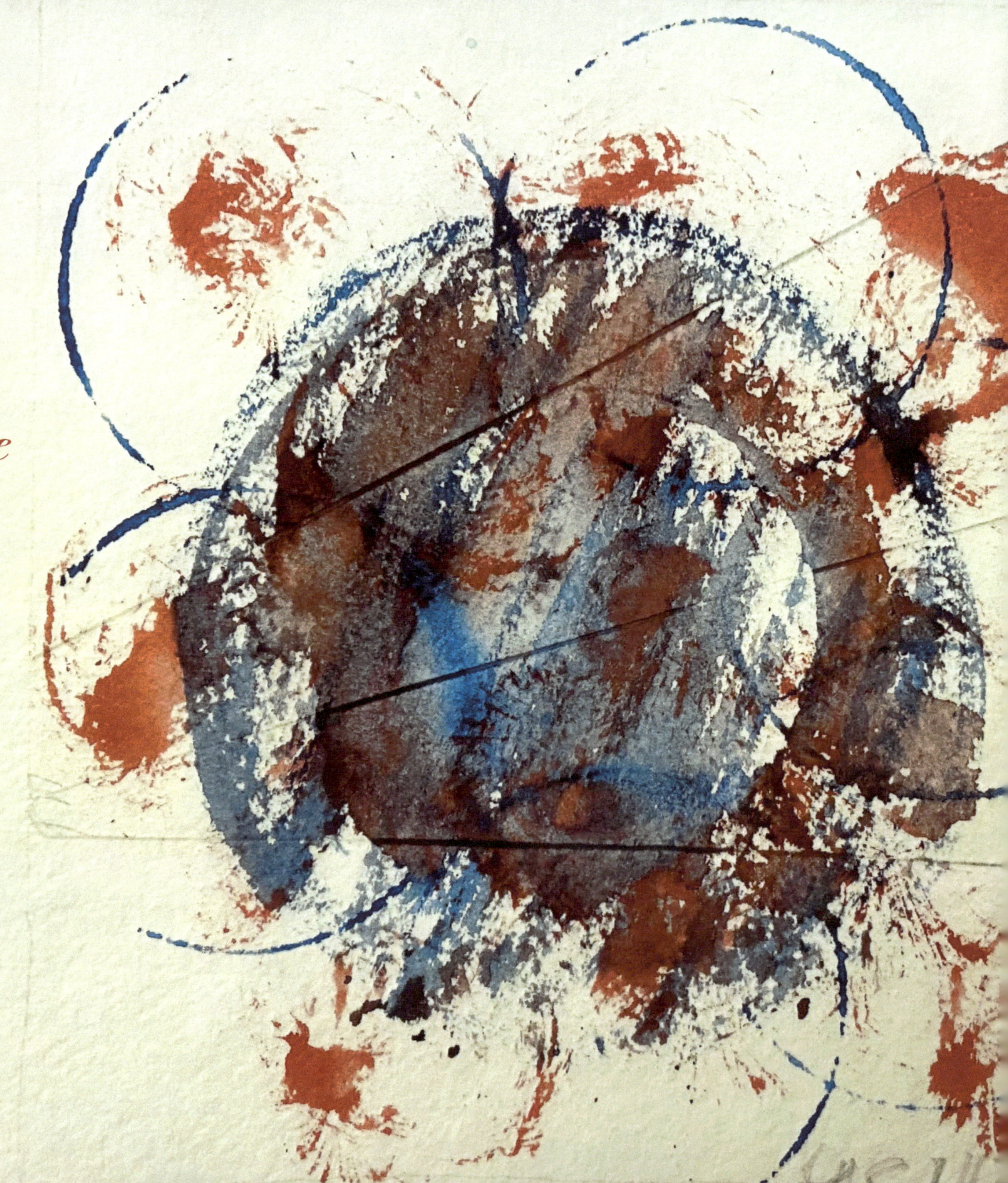

Summer Solstice '21

Messages
of balance
support me

My tribe
and ancestors
are close

Deep connections
surface
new healing
and sharing

Tears flow
and laughter

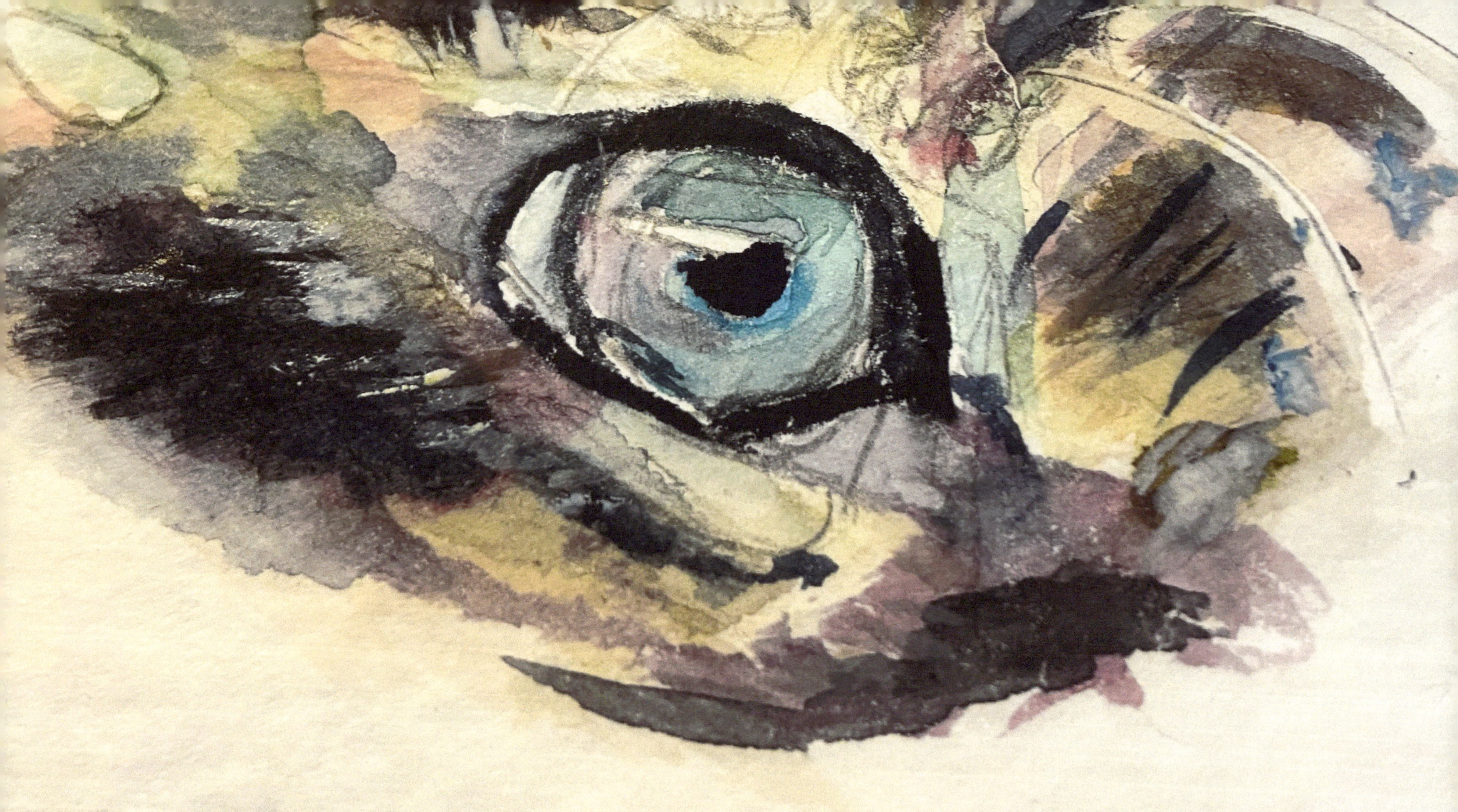

Eyes

Some eyes
dart and flash
and stab
trying to
eat you
in one eyeful

Others
bathe you
in a mirror-pond
drawing out
a strainless emotion

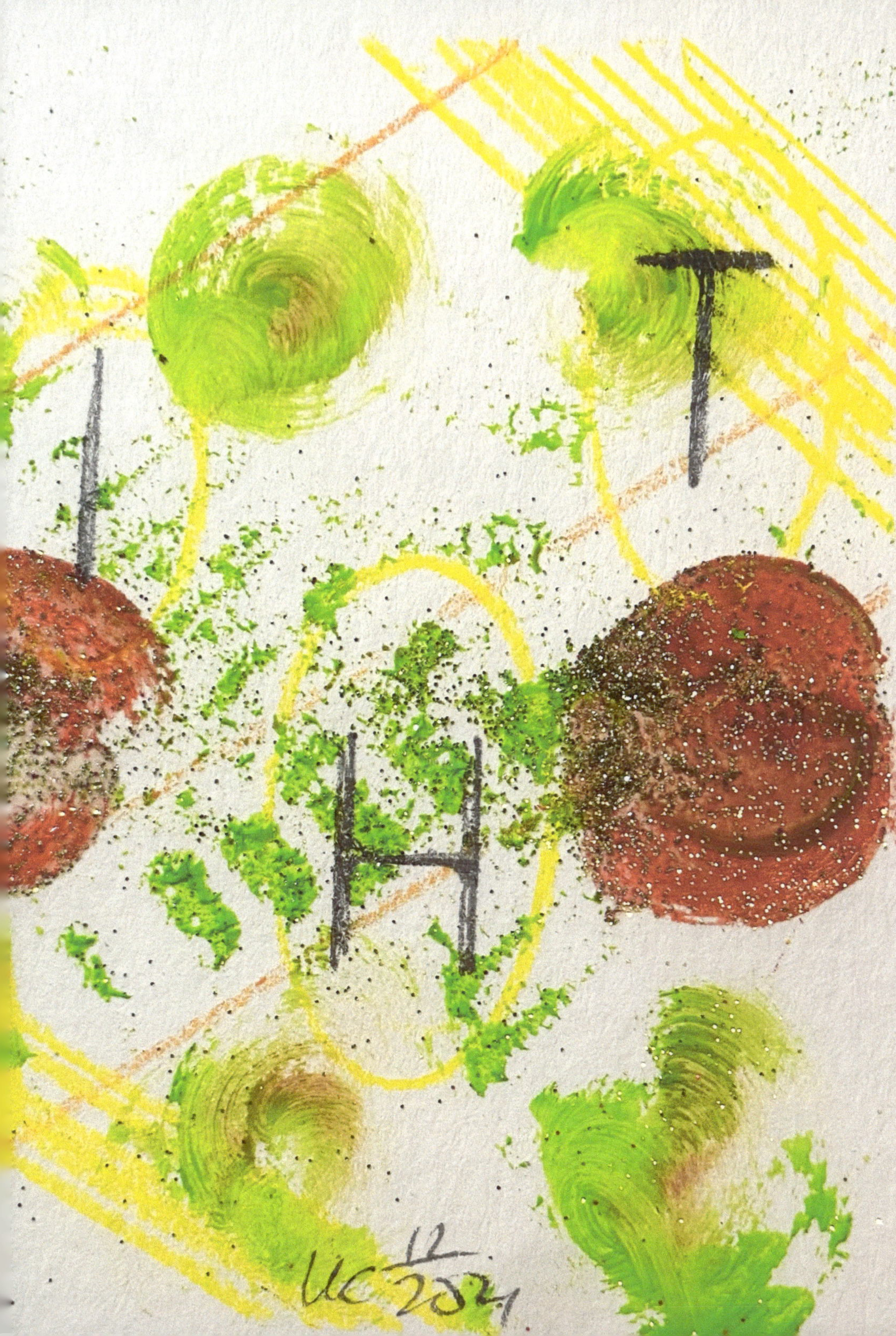

Love of My Life

Rescuer life-giver
and lover
co-creator of what
once seemed
an impossible
dream

Teacher of lightness
Reaching - out
and being
In the moment
laughter–machine
and fun-magnet

Passionate vocational
mother
with courage
to challenge
as well as support

Co-navigator through
loss and pain

Friend and
companion
with unique beauty
Inside and out

Love of my life
amen

One Evening

One evening
on the pier
A transcendent moment
as sea sky water and
clouds
shimmered and merged
into the spreading pink

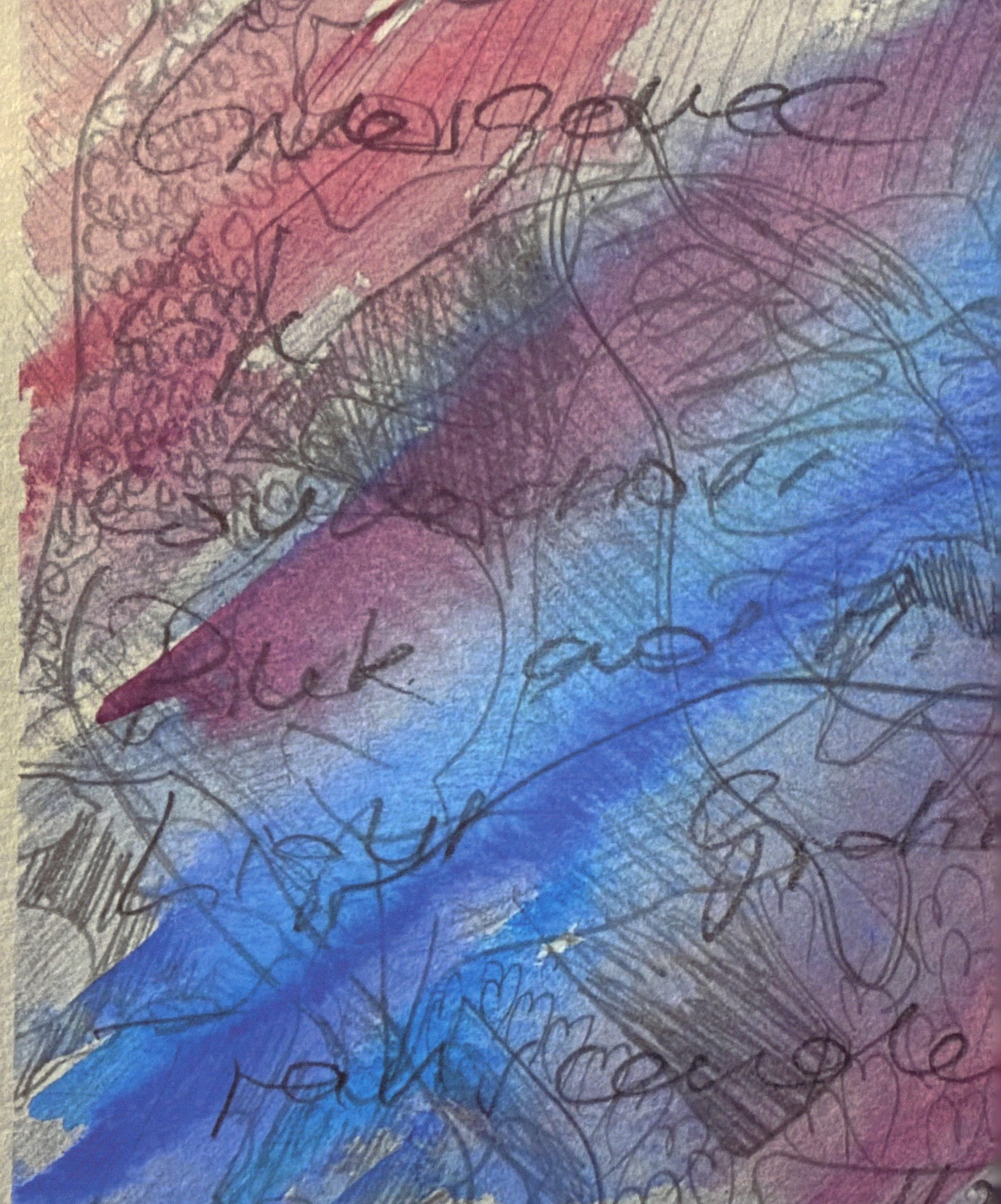

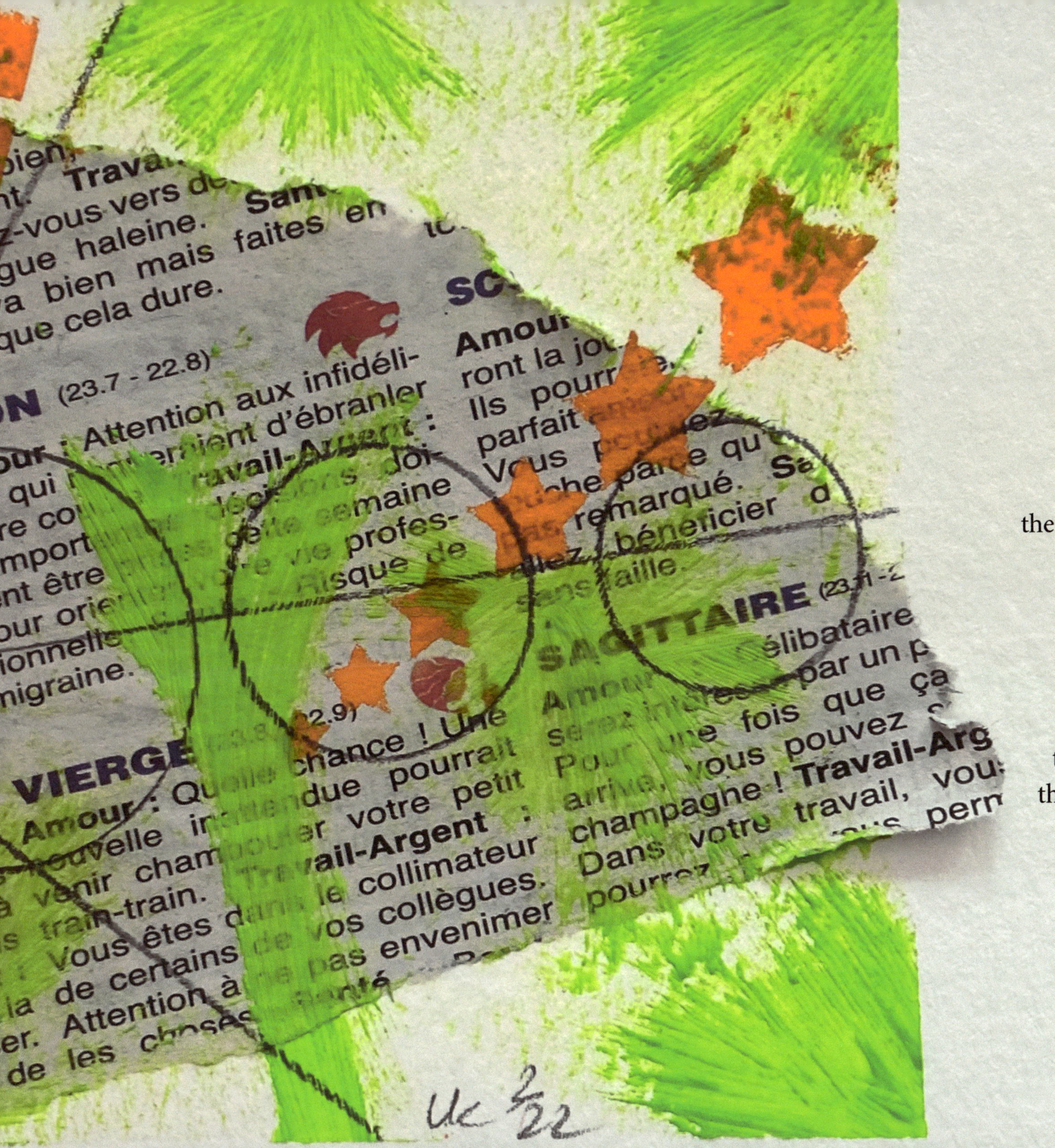

A Plan

A plan of love
was in my mind
a plan of giving all
I felt a change
and hoped
for so much more
for beauty and
the warmth of open doors
I thought I'd melt
the concrete
with the word

I looked again
and saw
the doors were open
the concrete was inside

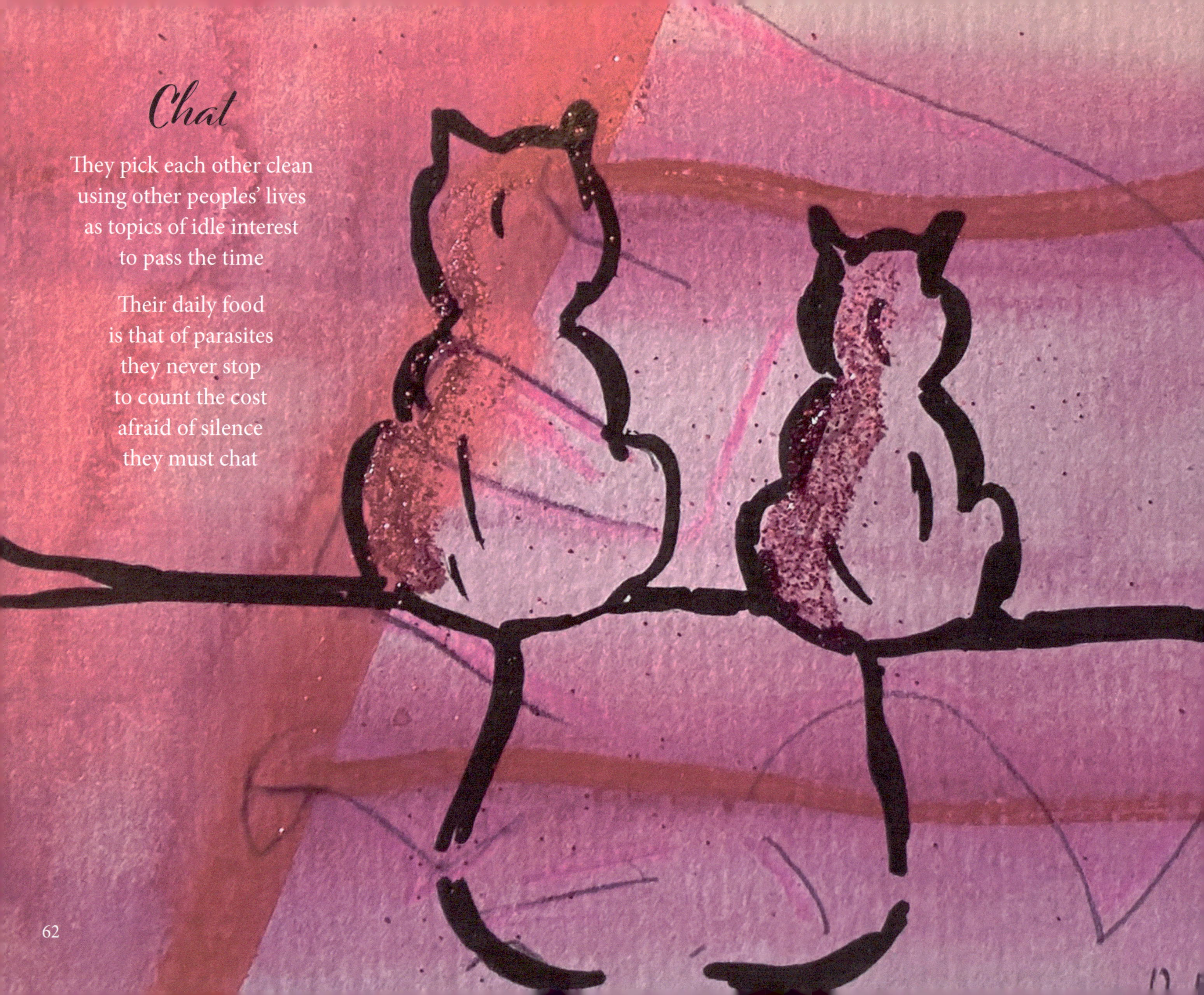

Chat

They pick each other clean
using other peoples' lives
as topics of idle interest
to pass the time

Their daily food
is that of parasites
they never stop
to count the cost
afraid of silence
they must chat

The Impeccable Practice of Truthfulness

So much is repressed
unspoken unexplored
so many limitations
are accepted
almost welcomed
as familiar companions

Truth and beauty
are intertwined
ugliness and hiding are also close
for truth to grow
we have to release
so much of self

Practice is everything
when we seek to access
the infinite potential
that is our gift

My Body

My present is so full now
my loving so complete
my heart my hands my feet
and all my body
feel so good now

Renewed restored refreshed
am I
so happy in myself
the mysteries
of love and life
have asked me in

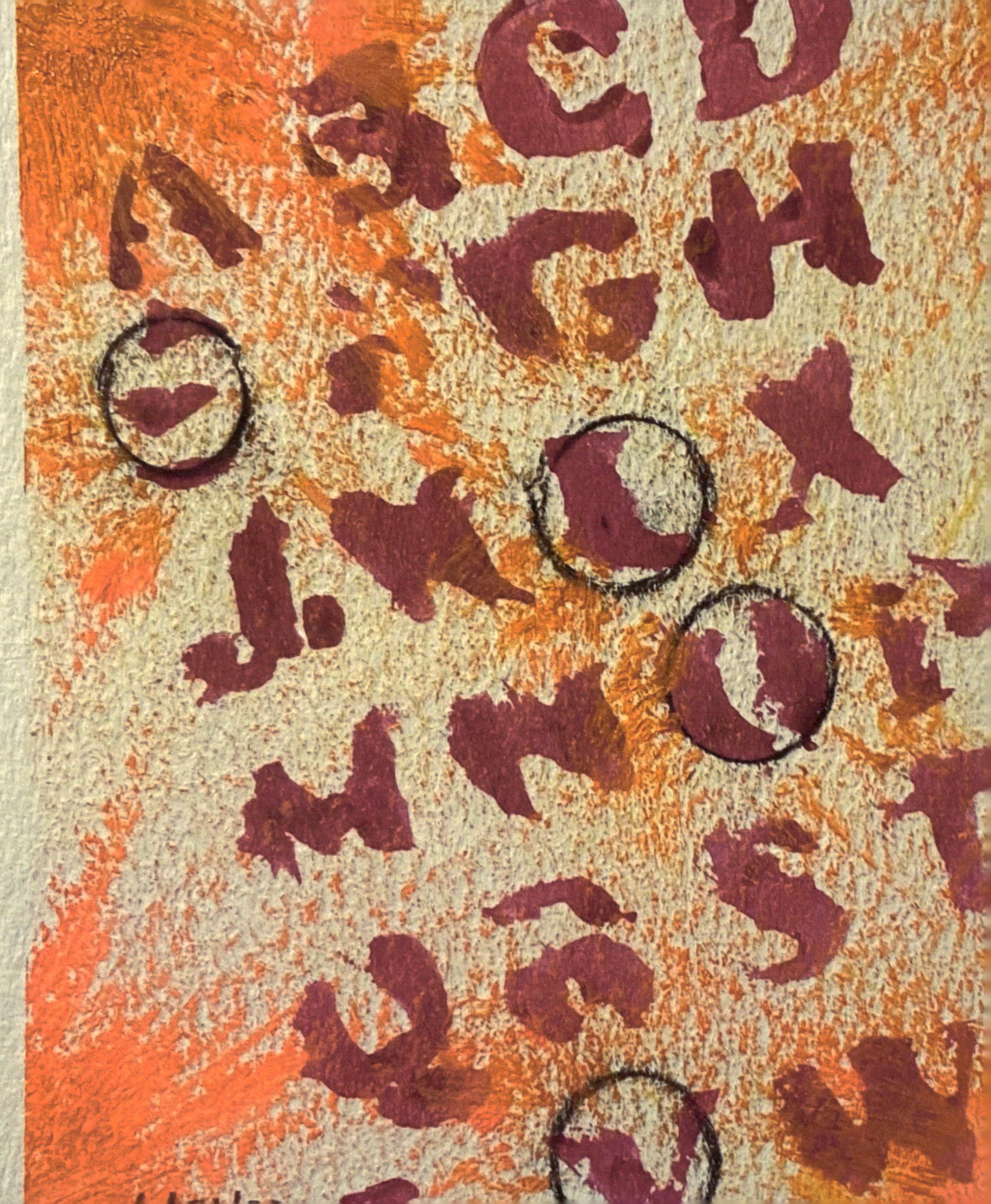

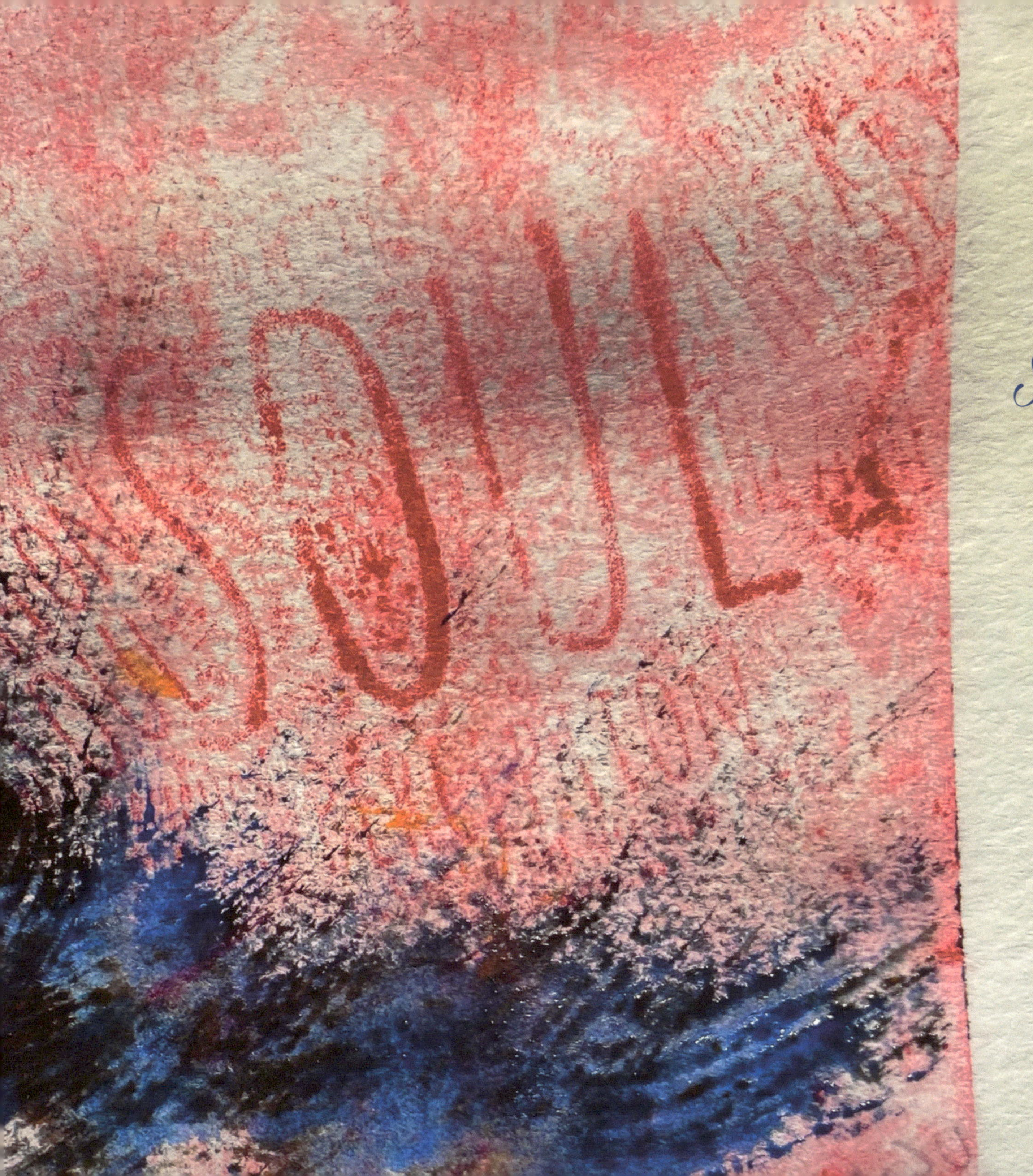

Soul Thoughts

Soul is shared
of the earth
sometimes beautiful
inspires and
connects

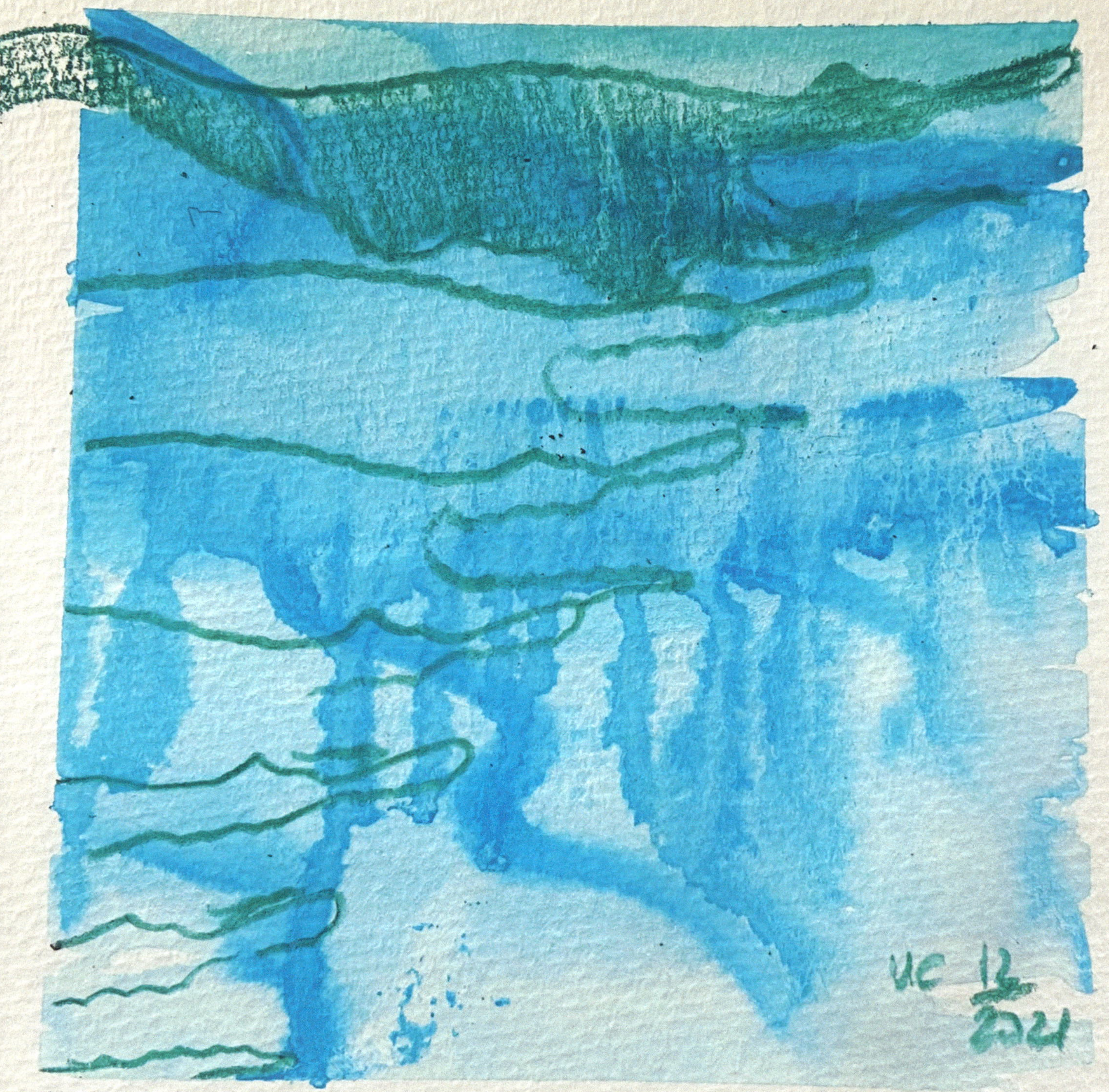

Seeking

The wells are full
the water's seeking
every crack and flaw
the eyes are floating
yet the liquid
does not cure my thirst
the emptiness inside expands
ready to burst
with the pressure of longing

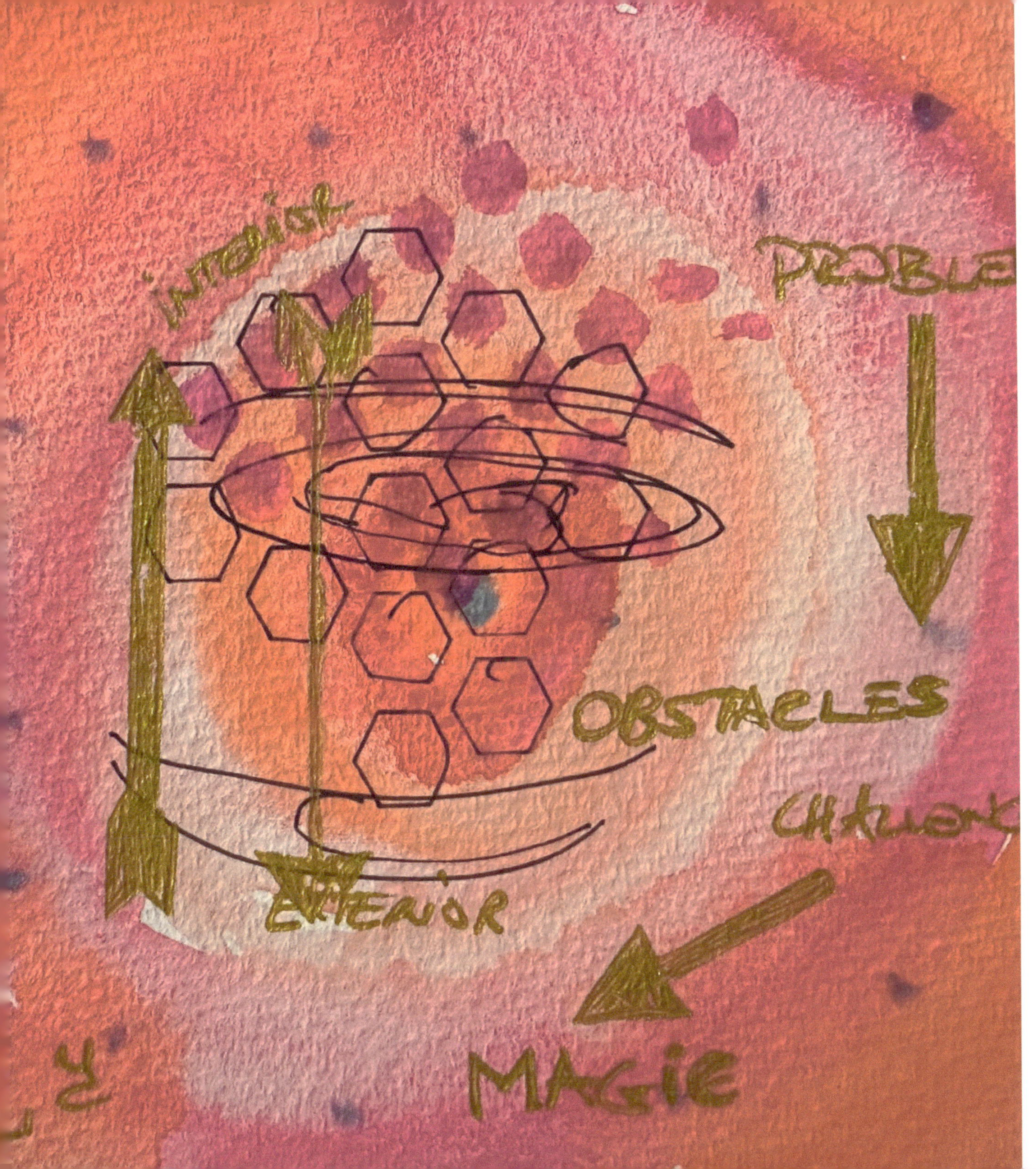

New Gain

New gain
from old pain
as I join the dots
of my life
so far

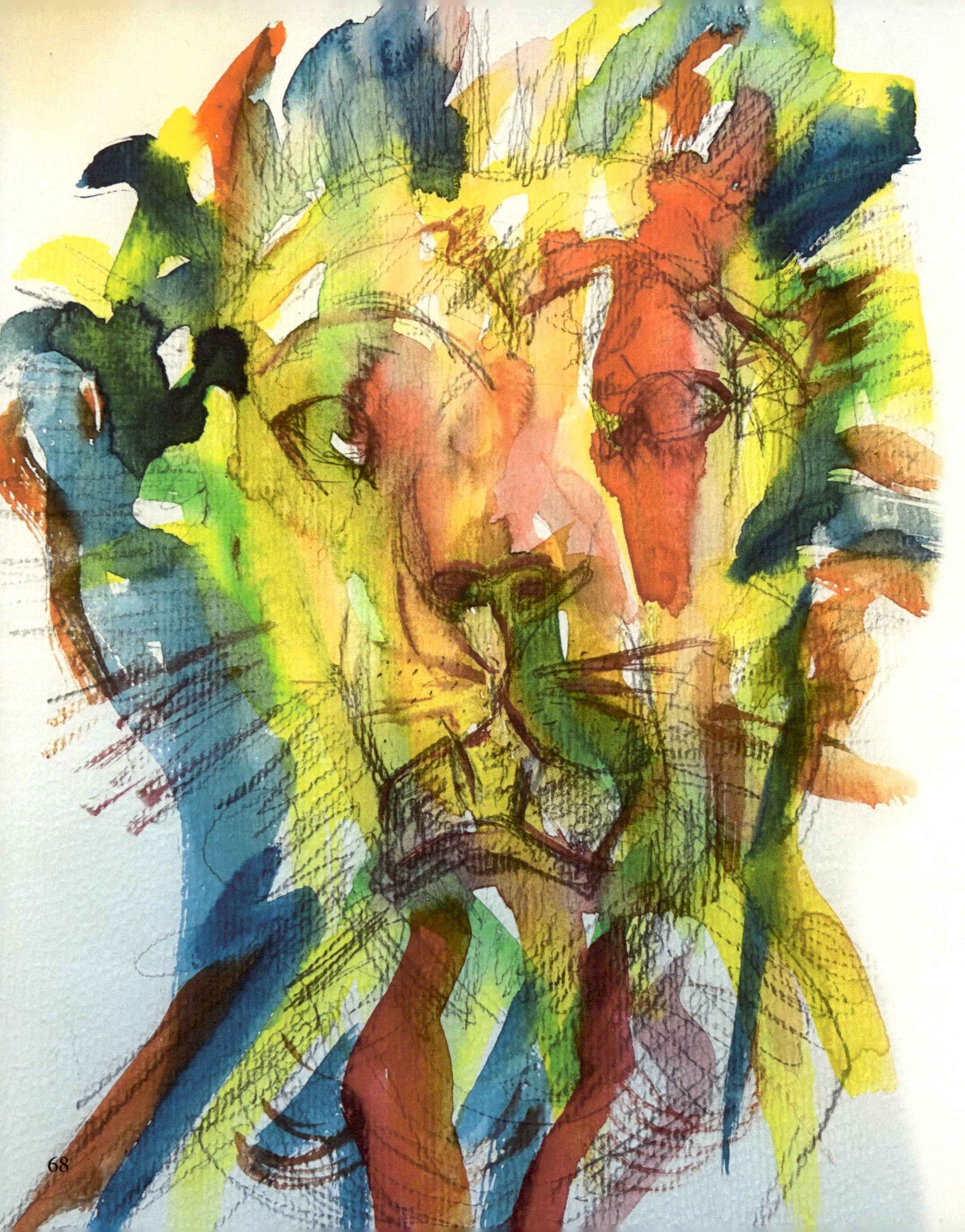

A Strength

A Strength once rejected
for its nakedness
and feared for its power
has now returned
to fill a thirsty pool
which another time
had cracked before its truth
and called it many names
to hide within a label
and live among the deadeners
of sympathy and pain
what use to bandage so a crack?
the pool remained empty

But now it fills through
that same crack
through which it emptied

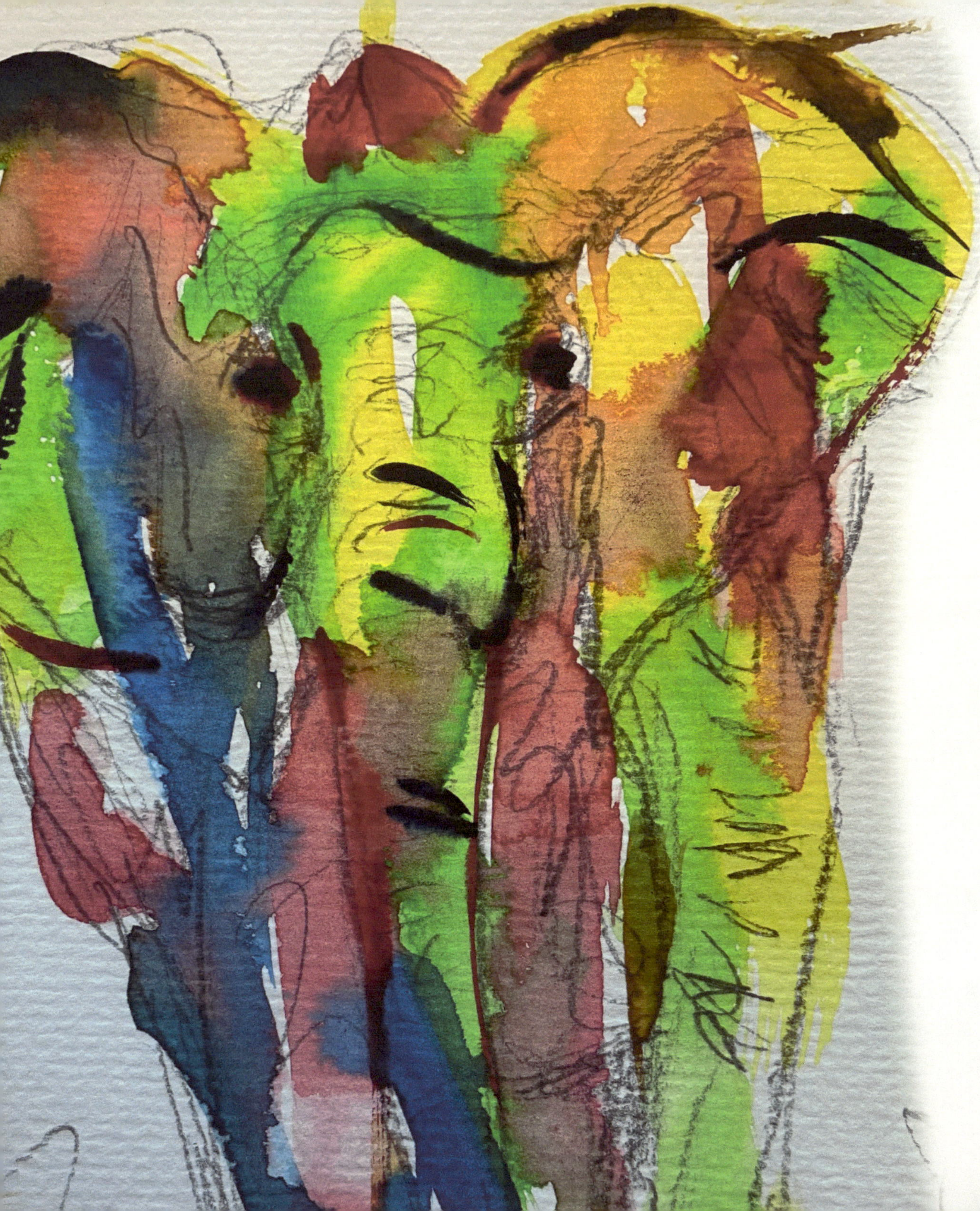

A Weight

My life has been
given back to me
the searing brand
of diagnosis
has been healed

I have recognised myself
and found my voice

As I begin to experience me
others have access
to the man
and the boy

My children know
my child for the
first time
We can all
move forward together

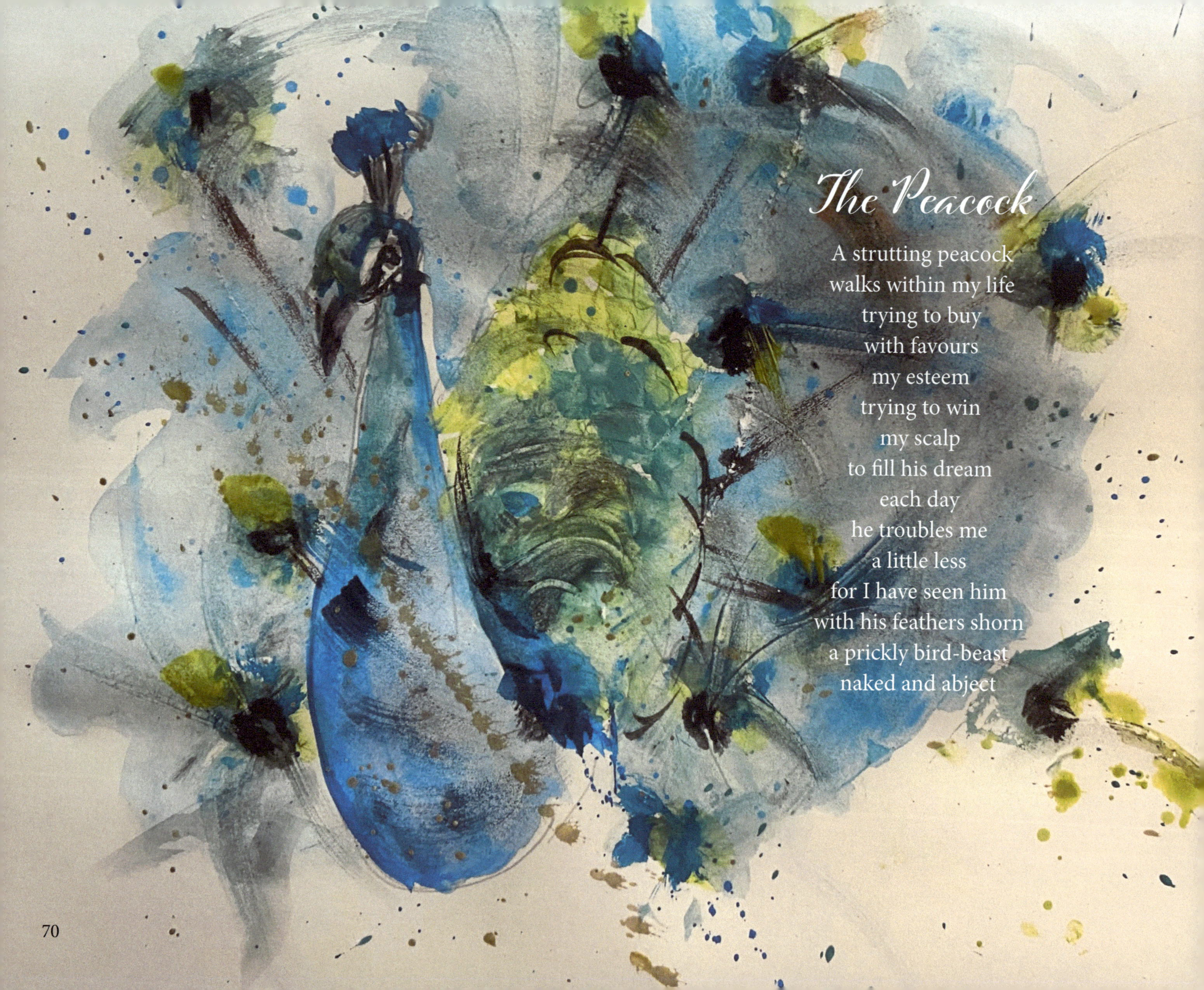

The Peacock

A strutting peacock
walks within my life
trying to buy
with favours
my esteem
trying to win
my scalp
to fill his dream
each day
he troubles me
a little less
for I have seen him
with his feathers shorn
a prickly bird-beast
naked and abject

70

Standing Tall

I am
learning to
stand tall
The lessons
are from
those I love

A straight back
and forward gaze
are more
than a
physical asset

They are a
psychological
epiphany

Whatever
made me
stoop
is lifting
as
my new
posture emerges

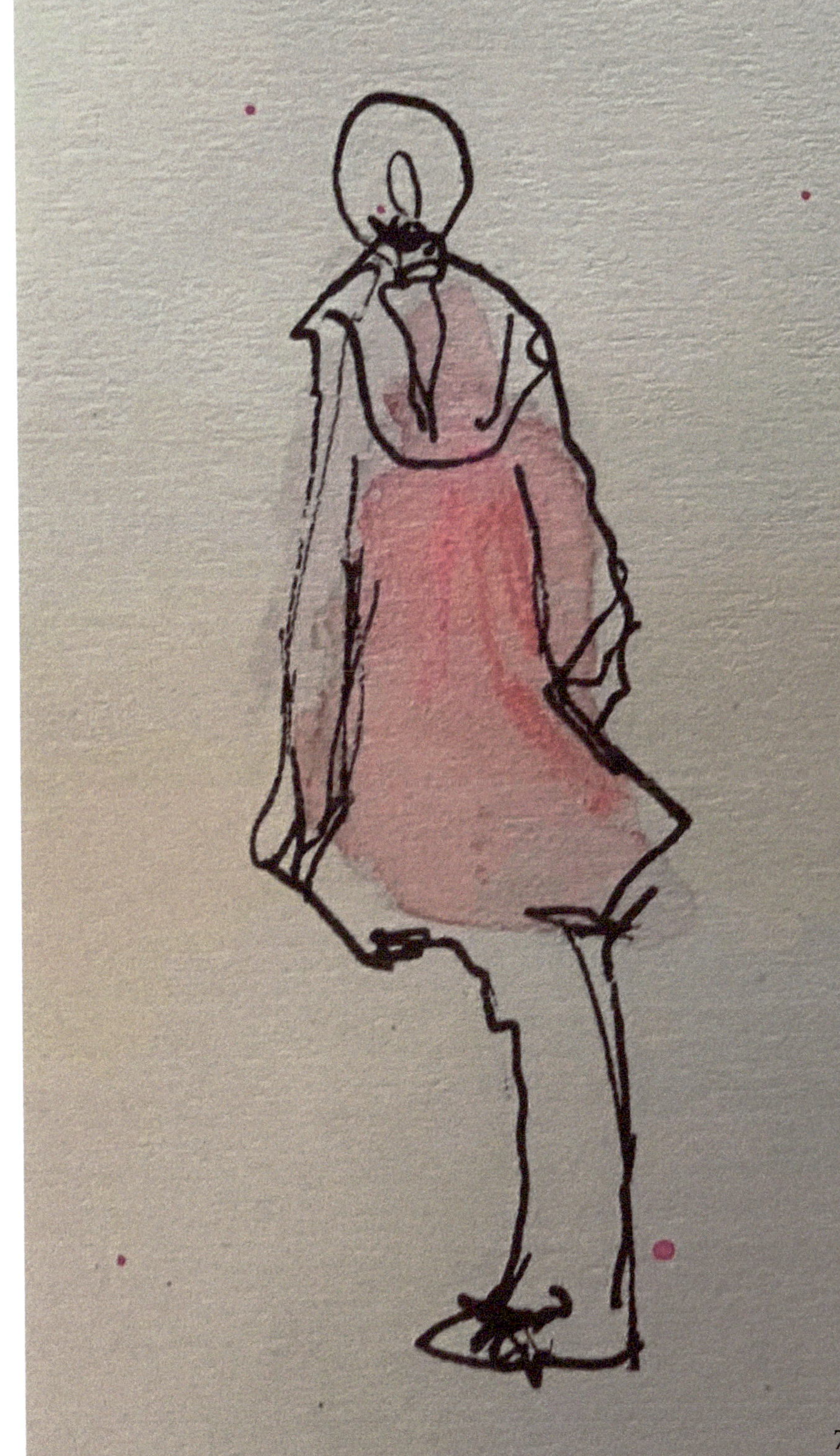

TOM FINLAY

As well as writing poetry, Tom acts as an independent director on
Financial services Companies, as an executive coach, a supervisor
of executive coaches, and as a psychotherapist. Tom's leisure
interests include, fly-fishing in the West of Ireland, Cycling, and
year-round sea-swimming.

URSULA CLIDIÈRE

Ursula has a corporate background and has spent most of her
career in a global Life Science company based in the US. She has a
doctorate in Organizational Psychology, worked as a Management
Consultant, then trained as Coach and Coach Supervisor. Many of
her leisure activities include the outdoors and sport.